PEARSON   ALWAYS LEARNING

Introduction to Project Management

with additional materials from SMC

Second Custom Edition for Santa Monica College

Taken from:
Project Management: Achieving Competitive Advantage, Second Edition
by Jeffrey K. Pinto

Cover Art: Courtesy of Photodisc/Getty Images.

Taken from:

Project Management: Achieving Competitive Advantage, Second Edition
by Jeffrey K. Pinto
Copyright © 2010, 2007 by Pearson Education, Inc.
Published by Prentice Hall
Upper Saddle River, New Jersey 07458

Pearson Learning Solutions, 501 Boylston Street, Suite 900, Boston, MA 02116
A Pearson Education Company
www.pearsoned.com

Printed in the United States of America

14 15 16 17 18 V0UD 19 18 17 16 15

000200010271672111

JH

ISBN 10: 1-256-78047-2
ISBN 13: 978-1-256-78047-2

TABLE OF CONTENTS

- **Overview of Project Management Concepts**   v
- **Project Management Presentation**   vii
- **Chapter 1—Introduction: Why Project Management?**   1
- **MyITLab Registration Instructions**   31

Overview of Project Management Concepts

Introduction to Project Management:

Project Management is about balancing time, budget and quality while achieving a final goal. The **project goal** is achieved when a series of tasks are completed. Every project must have a start and an end date.

The theory of Project Management is based on five processes that are usually in sequence and sometimes overlap. These five processes cover one or more knowledge areas.

The **five processes** include: Initiating, Planning, Executing, Monitoring and controlling, and Closing.

The **nine Knowledge Areas** include: Scope management, Time management, Cost management, Quality management, Human Resources management, Communication management, Risk management, Procurement, and Project Integration.

While running a project, a project manager first enters the Initiating process to get the project started. The project manager may write a proposal to get funding that also details the goals of the project. The project manager sets the schedule with an estimate of the total cost and time required to complete the project.

As the project progresses into planning, executing and other processes, the project manager applies one or more skills of the nine Knowledge Areas to ensure the successful completion of the project.

Every project is constrained by its scope (what work will be done), time (how long should it take to complete) and cost (how much should it cost). It is the project manager's duty to balance these three. These are referred to as the Triple Constraint. The Triple Constraint pulls the project manager in opposing directions. Recently, educators in this field added a forth constraint: Quality (how much does the final product meet expectations).

Benefits of Project Management:

- Better understanding of overall project goals and alignment with business objectives

- Better understanding of project tasks, duration, schedule dates, and costs

- More organized and streamlined way to manage the many details of a project

- More accurate and reliable project status information

- More efficient use of project resources

- Better communication among management, project managers, and other stakeholders

- Faster response to conflicting project goals

- Greater awareness of project processes

- Quicker project completion

- Lower project costs

- Fewer project failures

Project Managers are better equipped with the knowledge and tools to successfully deliver products on time.

Project Management Terminology:

You don't need to be an expert to understand some of the basic terms used in the theoretical study of Project Management and the application of MS Project. Here are a few key terms:

Task

A *task* is a specific action that needs to be completed in order to achieve the project goal. For example, if your goal is to remodel a kitchen (Project End Goal), one task might be "buy new appliances".

Duration

Each task has *duration*, or an amount of time required to finish the task.

Resources

Resources are the people, equipment, or facilities (such as contractors, trucks, paint, etc.) that need to be assigned to a task in order to complete it. Anything that costs money to apply to a task is a resource.

Stakeholder

A *stakeholder* is a person or entity that may indirectly be affected by a project or holds a positive or negative interest in a project.

Project Manager

The *project manager* is the central person who runs the project and ensures the timely execution of the project plan.

Scope

Scope is all the work involved in creating the products of the project and the processes used to create them. A clear project goal will help communicate the scope of the project. In other words, if you plan to remodel a kitchen, then a clear scope would exclude changing the entire house's flooring, and identifies in details what the remodeling involves.

Quality

Quality is the degree to which something meets an objective standard. Almost every project and task has implied quality standards. In a kitchen-remodeling project, the quality may be applied to the type of wood used in the cabinets, and which manufacturer produces them. Other criteria such as flooring type and type of installation are also included.

Project Milestone

A *project milestone* is a task that marks a significant point in time or a progress checkpoint. Remodeling a kitchen may have finishing the floor, installing cabinets, and delivering appliances as milestones. A milestone has zero duration, since it requires no cost in general.

Project Management Software

One of the leading software tools in Project Management is MS Project.

The GANTT chart is the most common view in MS Project for reviewing a project and was first used in a drawing in 1917.

Project Management Certification and Education:

A certification in Project Management requires the detailed study of the five processes and where they overlap, using the nine Knowledge Areas.

An experienced Project Manager uses the nine Knowledge Areas to produce schedules and plans to run the project at hand to its final goal, with a high degree of success.

The Project Management Institute is an authority in the formal study and profession of Project Management and offers certification in Project Management.

Proven Results show that PM in the field is 'for real'

- With over 18% of IT projects failing or getting canceled due to bad management and only 29% succeeding in reaching their original goal, many organizations today have a new or renewed interest in project management.(The Standish Group, "Chaos 2001: A Recipe for Success" 2001)

- The Great Wall of China was one of the first projects on Earth.

- Most people consider the Manhattan Project to be the first project to use "modern" project management theory. This three-year, $2 billion (in 1946 dollars) project had separate project and technical managers.

PROJECT MANAGEMENT

- What is it?
- Why should I care?
- How can I learn it?

PROJECT MANAGEMENT IS ONE OF THE FASTEST GROWING PROFESSIONS IN THE U.S.

Project Managers work in information technology as well as construction and other industries.

Project Managers are among the top 10 highly paid professionals. Their positions do not get subcontracted to overseas. Demand is high in the U.S. according to statistics from www.pimi.org-Salary Survey 2005.

HOW HAS PROJECT MANAGEMENT RECENTLY EMERGED?

- The U.S. spends one-quarter of its gross domestic product on projects of all kinds. This tells you about the potential for the project management field. (www.pmi.org Fact Book Second Edition 2001)

- With over 18% of IT projects failing or getting canceled due to bad management and only 29% succeeding in reaching their original goal, many organizations today have a new or renewed interest in project management. (The Standish Group, "Chaos 2001: A Recipe for Success" 2001)

- Could you be the next sought after Project Manager?

HISTORY OF PROJECT MANAGEMENT

- Some people argue that building the Egyptian pyramids was a project, as was the Great Wall of China.

- Most people consider the **Manhattan Project** to be the first project to use "modern" project management theory.

  - This three-year, $2 billion (in 1946 dollars) project had a separate project and technical manager.

ADVANTAGES OF USING FORMAL PROJECT MANAGEMENT

◎ Project Managers are better equipped with the knowledge and tools to successfully deliver products on time.

◎ This keeps the customers happy and improves customer relations.

◎ The overall cost will be lower and a timely delivery is more feasible.

◎ This reduces stress at the workplace and increases morale.

BUT WHAT IS A PROJECT?

So working in a certain job is not a project. Developing a car, however, is a project. The key is that a project is temporary and has a start and end.

◎ A **project** is "a temporary endeavor undertaken to create a unique product, service, or result."

◎ The nature of work done is to support the business goals.

◎ A project ends when its objectives have been reached, or the project has been terminated.

◎ Projects can be large or small and take a short or long time to complete.

EXAMPLES OF PROJECTS

◎ A cross-functional task force in a company **decides what software** to purchase and how it will be implemented.

◎ A television network **develops a system** to allow viewers to vote for contestants and provide other feedback on programs.

◎ A government group **develops a system** to track child immunizations.

PROJECT ATTRIBUTES

So, improving humanity, even though a noble cause, does not qualify as a purpose because it is not temporary (no begin and end date – a lifelong struggle).

A project:

⊙ Has a unique purpose.

⊙ Is temporary.

⊙ Is developed using progressive elaboration.

⊙ Requires resources, often from various areas.

⊙ Should have a primary customer or sponsor:

○ The **project sponsor** usually provides the direction and funding for the project.

⊙ Involves uncertainty or risk.

PROJECT STAKEHOLDERS

Stakeholders are the people involved in or affected by project activities.

- Stakeholders include:
  - Project sponsor
  - Project manager
  - Project team
  - Support staff
  - Customers
  - Users
  - Suppliers
  - Opponents to the project

- As an example, Santa Monica College has a 'big' project at hand, and that is to educate the public. Who are the Stakeholders?

- Identifying the stakeholders identifies who is impacted by the project. For example, if I want to teach a certain class, it is important to know who the stakeholders are, otherwise I risk not being able to offer the class or not having students sign up for it. The 'important' stakeholders are the Students and the Administration.

- Stakeholders are categorized. The higher the 'stakes', the more we need to include that stakeholder in our goals.

STAKEHOLDERS MAY HAVE POSITIVE (+) OR NEGATIVE (-) INTEREST

For example, the residents of a neighborhood may resist a project nearby to transform the local park into a parking lot.

- They do not want to lose the park, and therefore will resist the development.

- The residents are considered negative stakeholders.

- A similar example would be competitors in most business models.

HOW A PROJECT STARTS

A customer says "I want you to build me an Accounting System".

◎ You write a proposal (and possibly create a demo).

◎ List the objectives and goals that will be achieved at the end.

◎ If you get the proposal, you 'estimate' the time and the cost of the system. Later you 'control' the scope of the project to ensure you develop what you promised, no more or less.

◎ Project management gives you the tools and techniques to estimate and communicate the cost, time and scope of the project, among other parameters. These techniques and tools are referred to as Knowledge Areas.

NINE PROJECT MANAGEMENT KNOWLEDGE AREAS

Knowledge areas describe the key skills that project managers must develop.

⊙ Four core knowledge areas control and manage the scope, time, cost, and quality.

⊙ Four facilitating knowledge areas are the means through which the project objectives are achieved, namely human resources, communication, risk, and procurement management.

⊙ One knowledge area , project integration management, affects and is affected by all of the other knowledge areas.

⊙ All knowledge areas are important!

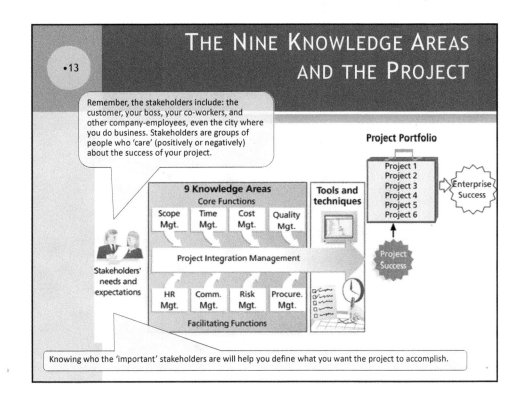

THE NINE KNOWLEDGE AREAS AND THE PROJECT

•13

Remember, the stakeholders include: the customer, your boss, your co-workers, and other company-employees, even the city where you do business. Stakeholders are groups of people who 'care' (positively or negatively) about the success of your project.

Knowing who the 'important' stakeholders are will help you define what you want the project to accomplish.

THE TRIPLE CONSTRAINT

•14

- Every project is constrained in different ways by its:

  - Scope goals: What work will be done?

  - Time goals: How long should it take to complete?

  - Cost goals: How much should it cost?

- It is the project manager's duty to balance these three often-competing criterion and *meet the Sponsor's goal.*

IMAGINE YOU BEING PULLED IN 3 OPPOSING DIRECTIONS. THAT'S THE TRIPLE CONSTRAINT IN PROJECT MANAGEMENT.

•15

THREE OR FOUR CONSTRAINTS?

•16

◎ In recent years, some educators in project management assert that another level of constraint affects a project.

◎ This forth level is **Quality**: Does the final product meet expectations?

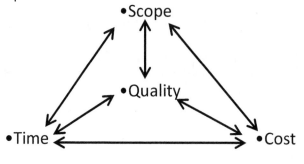

•Scope

•Quality

•Time   •Cost

IN SHORT...

•17

◎ **Project management** is "the application of knowledge, skills, tools and techniques to project activities to meet project requirements".

ROLES OF A PROJECT MANAGER

•18

◎ Job descriptions vary, but most include responsibilities such as planning, scheduling, coordinating, and working with people to achieve project goals.

◎ 97% of successful projects were led by experienced project managers.

Suggested Skills for Project Managers

•19

- Communication **skills**: Listen and persuade.

- Organizational **skills**: Plan, sets goal, analyze.

- Team-building **skills**: Show empathy, motivate, promote esprit de corps.

- Leadership **skills**: Set examples, provide vision (big picture), delegate, be positive, energetic.

- Coping **skills**: Flexible, creative, patient, persistent.

- Technology **skills**: Experience, project knowledge.

Project Management Software

•20

- There are currently hundreds of different products to assist in performing project management.

- Three main categories of tools:

  - Low-end tools: Handle single or smaller projects well; cost under $200 per user.

  - Mid-range tools: Handle multiple projects and users; cost $200-500 per user; Microsoft Project is the most popular.

  - High-end tools: Also called enterprise project management software; often licensed on a per-user basis.

MICROSOFT PROJECT

◎ Has many editions to suit small scale to large scale projects and enterprises.

◎ Has tools needed to manage budget, track progress and assign and group human resources and equipment.

◎ Installs under Microsoft Office.

GANTT CHART:
A POPULAR VIEW IN MS PROJECT

- Gantt charts are how projects are viewed in MS Project.
- The spreadsheet on left lists project tasks and the graph on right shows how tasks are related and the start and end dates.
- First used in 1917, early Gantt charts were drawn by hand.

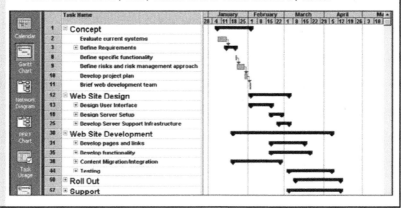

THE PROJECT MANAGEMENT PROFESSION

- Professional societies such as the Project Management Institute (PMI) have grown significantly.

- There are specific interest groups in many areas, such as engineering, financial services, health care, and IT.

- Project management research and certification programs continue to grow.

- The CSIS department offers two certificates in Project Management.

PROJECT MANAGEMENT INSTITUTE

- Visit www.pmi.org for details on certification.

- To earn credit hours you may sign up for CS/CIS 9A or 9B.

- The two courses above, also help you prepare for the certification exam.

- Visit www.smc.edu/csis/pm for details on Project Management certificates that the CSIS department offers at SMC.

PROJECT MANAGEMENT CERTIFICATION

PMI provides certification as a Project Management Professional (PMP).

- The number of people earning PMP certification is increasing quickly.

- To get certified you need to earn credit hours by taking PM courses, passing the PMP exam and showing, through experience, that you will follow a code of ethics.

- Other certifications that do not require experience are also available, such as CAPM.

PROJECT MANAGEMENT STUDY

- Project Management is a rising field of study and applies to other areas of study.

- Project Managers study the nine Knowledge Areas, among other management concepts.

- Certification in Project Management is valuable.

- The PMI offers PMP and CAPM certification; the first requires experience, the second does not

- SMC offers its own certification.

Introduction
Why Project Management?

Chapter Outline

PROJECT PROFILE
    Case—Disney's Expedition Everest
INTRODUCTION
1.1 WHAT IS A PROJECT?
    General Project Characteristics
1.2 WHY ARE PROJECTS IMPORTANT?
PROJECT PROFILE
    Dubai—Land of Mega-Projects
1.3 PROJECT LIFE CYCLES
PROJECT MANAGERS IN PRACTICE
    Christy Rutkowski, Regency Construction Services
1.4 DETERMINANTS OF PROJECT SUCCESS
PROJECT MANAGEMENT RESEARCH IN BRIEF
    Assessing Information Technology (IT) Project Success
1.5 DEVELOPING PROJECT MANAGEMENT MATURITY
1.6 PROJECT ELEMENTS AND TEXT ORGANIZATION
Summary
Key Terms
Discussion Questions
Case Study 1.1 MegaTech, Inc.
Case Study 1.2 The IT Department at Hamelin Hospital
Internet Exercises
PMP Certification Sample Questions
Notes

Chapter Objectives

After completing this chapter you should be able to:

1. Understand why project management is becoming such a powerful and popular practice in business.
2. Recognize the basic properties of projects, including their definition.

3. Understand why effective project management is such a challenge.

4. Differentiate between project management practices and more traditional, process-oriented business functions.

5. Recognize the key motivators that are pushing companies to adopt project management practices.

6. Understand and explain the project life cycle, its stages, and the activities that typically occur at each stage in the project.

7. Understand the concept of project "success," including various definitions of success, as well as the alternative models of success.

8. Understand the purpose of project management maturity models and the process of benchmarking in organizations.

9. Identify the relevant maturity stages that organizations go through to become proficient in their use of project management techniques.

PROJECT MANAGEMENT BODY OF KNOWLEDGE CORE CONCEPTS COVERED IN THIS CHAPTER

1. Definition of a Project (PMBoK sec. 1.2)

2. Definition of Project Management (PMBoK sec. 1.3)

3. Relationship to Other Management Disciplines (PMBoK sec. 1.4)

4. Project Phases and the Project Life Cycle (PMBoK sec. 2.1)

The world acquires value only through its extremes and endures only through moderation; extremists make the world great, the moderates give it stability.[1]

PROJECT PROFILE

Case—Disney's Expedition Everest

The newest thrill ride to open in the Walt Disney World Resort may just be the most impressive. As Disney approached its 50th anniversary, the company wanted to celebrate in a truly special way. Their idea? Create a park attraction that would, in many ways, serve as the link between Disney's amazing past and its promising future. In getting everything just right, Disney showed that it was ready to pull out all the stops.

In 2006, The Walt Disney Company introduced Expedition Everest in Disney's Animal Kingdom Park at Lake Buena Vista, Florida. Expedition Everest is more than just a roller coaster. It is the embodiment of the Disney spirit: a ride that combines Disney's trademark thrills, unexpected twists and turns, incredible attention to detail, and impressive project management skills.

First, let's consider some of the technical details of Expedition Everest:

- With a peak of just under 200 feet, the ride is contained within the tallest of 18 mountains created by Disney's Imagineers at Disney parks worldwide.
- The ride contains nearly a mile of track, with twists, tight turns, and sudden drops.
- The Disney team created a Yeti: an enormous, fur-covered, Audio-Animatronics monster powered by a set of hydraulic cylinders whose combined thrust equals that of a Boeing 747 airliner. Through a series of sketches, computer-animated drawings, sculptures, and tests that took over two years to perfect, Disney created and programmed its Abominable Snowman to stand over 10 feet tall and serve as the focal point of the ride.
- More than 900 bamboo plants, 10 species of trees, and 110 species of shrubs were planted to re-create the feeling of the Himalayan lowlands surrounding Mount Everest.
- Over 1,800 tons of steel were used to construct the mountain. The covering of the framework was done using more than 3,000 pre-fabricated "chips" created from 25,000 individual computer-molded pieces of steel.

- To create the proper color schemes, 2,000 gallons of stain and paint were used on rockwork and throughout the village Disney created to serve as a backdrop for the ride.
- More than 2,000 handcrafted items from Asia are used as props, cabinetry, and architectural ornamentation.

Building an attraction does not come easily or quickly for Disney's Imagineers. Expedition Everest was several years in development as Disney sent teams, including Walt Disney Imagineering's Creative Executive Joe Rohde, on repeated trips to the Himalayas in Nepal to study the lands, architecture, colors, ecology, and culture in order to create the most authentic setting for the new attraction. Disney's efforts reflect a desire to do much more than provide a world-class ride experience; they demonstrate the Imagineers' eagerness to tell a story—a story that combines the mythology of the Yeti figure with the unique history of the Nepalese living in the shadow of the world's tallest mountain. Ultimately, the attraction, with all its background and thematic elements, took nearly five years to complete.

Riders on Expedition Everest gain a real feel for the atmosphere that Disney has worked so hard to create. The guests' adventure starts by entering the building of the "Himalayan Escape" tour company, complete with Norbu and Bob's booking office to obtain permits for their trip. Overhead flutter authentic prayer flags from monasteries in Nepal. Next, guests pass through Tashi's General Store and Bar to stock up on supplies for their journey to the peak of the mountain. Finally, guests pass through an old tea warehouse that contains a remarkable museum of artifacts reflecting Nepal's culture, a history of the Himalayas, and tales of the Yeti, which is said to inhabit the slopes of Mount Everest. It is only now that guests are permitted to board the Anandapur Rail Service for their trip to the peak. Each train is modeled after an aging, steam-engine train, seating 34 guests per train.

Over the next several minutes, guests are transported up the roller coaster track, through a series of winding turns, until their encounter with the Yeti. It is at this point that another unique feature of the attraction emerges; the train begins rushing backward down the track, as though it were out of control. Through the balance of the ride, guests experience a landscape of sights and sounds culminating in a 50 mph final dash down the mountain and back to the safety of the Nepalese village.

Disney's approach to the management of projects such as Expedition Everest is to combine careful planning, including schedule and budget preparation, with the imagination and vision for which the company is so well known. Creativity is a critical element in the development of new projects at Disney. Their Imagineers include some

FIGURE 1.1   **Disney's Expedition Everest**

(continued)

of the most skilled artists and computer-animation experts in the world. While it is easy to be impressed by the technical knowledge of Disney's personnel, it is also important to remember that each new project is approached with an understanding of their underlying business, including market projections, cost control, and attention to careful project management discipline. New attraction proposals are carefully screened and researched. The result is the creation of some of the most innovative and enjoyable rides in the world. Disney does not add new attractions to their theme parks frequently, but when it does so, it does it with style![2]

INTRODUCTION

Projects are one of the principal means by which we change our world. Whether the goal is to split the atom, tunnel under the English Channel, introduce Windows Vista, or plan the next Olympic games in London, the means to achieve all these tasks remains the same: through project management. Project management has become one of the most popular tools for organizations, both public and private, to improve internal operations, respond rapidly to external opportunities, achieve technological breakthroughs, streamline new product development, and more robustly manage the challenges arising from their business environment. Consider what Tom Peters, best-selling author and management consultant, has to say about project management and its place in business: "Projects, rather than repetitive tasks, are now the basis for most value-added in business."[3] Project management has become a critical component of successful business operations in worldwide organizations.

One of the key features of modern business is the nature of the opportunities and threats posed by external events. As never before, companies face international competition and the need to pursue commercial opportunities rapidly. They must modify and introduce products constantly, respond to customers as fast as possible, and maintain competitive cost and operating levels. Does performing all these tasks seem impossible? At one time, it was. Conventional wisdom held that a company could compete using a low-cost strategy *or* as a product innovator *or* with a focus on customer service. In short, we had to pick our competitive niches and concede others their claim to market share. In the 1990s, however, everything turned upside down. Companies such as General Electric, Nokia, Ericksson, Boeing, and Oracle became increasingly good at realizing all of these goals rather than settling for just one. These companies seemed to be successful in every aspect of the competitive model: They were fast to market *and* efficient, cost conscious *and* customer-focused. How were they performing the impossible?

Obviously, there is no one answer to this complex question. There is no doubt, however, that these companies shared at least one characteristic: They had developed and committed themselves to project management as a competitive tool. Old middle managers, reported *Fortune* magazine,

> are dinosaurs, [and] a new class of manager mammal is evolving to fill the niche they once ruled: project managers. Unlike his biological counterpart, the project manager is more agile and adaptable than the beast he's displacing, more likely to live by his wits than throwing his weight around.[4]

Effective project managers will remain an indispensable commodity for successful organizations in the coming years. More and more companies are coming to the same conclusion and adopting project management as a way of life. Indeed, companies in such diverse industries as construction, heavy manufacturing, insurance, health care, finance, public utilities, and software are all becoming project savvy and expecting their employees to do the same.

1.1 WHAT IS A PROJECT?

Although there are a number of general definitions of the term **project,** we must recognize at the outset that projects are distinct from other organizational processes. As a rule, a **process** refers to ongoing, day-to-day activities in which an organization engages while producing goods or services. Processes use existing systems, properties, and capabilities in a continuous, fairly repetitive manner.[5] Projects, on the other hand, take place outside the normal, process-oriented world of the firm. Certainly, in some organizations, such as construction, day-to-day processes center on the creation and development of projects. Nevertheless, for the majority of organizations, project management activities remain unique and separate from the manner in which more routine, process-driven work is performed. Project work is continuously evolving, establishes its own work rules, and is the antithesis of repetition in the workplace. As a result, it represents an exciting alternative to business as usual for many companies. The challenges are great, but so are the rewards of success.

First, we need a clear understanding of the properties that make projects and project management so unique. Consider the following definitions of projects:

> A project is a unique venture with a beginning and end, conducted by people to meet established goals within parameters of cost, schedule, and quality.[6]

> Projects [are] goal-oriented, involve the coordinated undertaking of interrelated activities, are of finite duration, and are all, to a degree, unique.[7]

> A project can be considered to be any series of activities and tasks that:
> - Have a specific objective to be completed within certain specifications
> - Have defined start and end dates
> - Have funding limits (if applicable)
> - Consume human and nonhuman resources (i.e., money, people, equipment)
> - Are multifunctional (i.e., cut across several functional lines)[8]

> Organized work toward a predefined goal or objective that requires resources and effort, a unique (and therefore risky) venture having a budget and schedule.[9]

Probably the simplest definition is found in the Project Management Body of Knowledge (PMBoK) guide of the Project Management Institute (PMI). PMI is the world's largest professional project management association, with more than 275,000 members worldwide as of 2008. In the PMBoK guide, a project is defined as "a temporary endeavor undertaken to create a unique product or service" (p. 4).[10]

Let us examine the various elements of projects, as identified by our set of definitions.

- *Projects are complex, one-time processes.* A project arises for a specific purpose or to meet a stated goal. They are complex because they typically require the coordinated inputs of numerous members of the organization. Project members may be from different departments or other organizational units or from one functional area. For example, a project to develop a new software application for a retail company may only require the output of members of the Information Systems group working with the marketing staff. On the other hand, some projects, such as new product introductions, work best with representation from many functions, including marketing, engineering, production, and design. Because a project is intended to fulfill a stated goal, it is temporary. It exists only until its goal has been met, and at that point, it is dissolved.
- *Projects are limited by budget, schedule, and resources.* Project work requires that members work with limited financial and human resources for a specified time period. They do not run indefinitely. Once the assignment is completed, the project team disbands. Until that point, all its activities are constrained by limitations on budget and personnel availability. Projects are "resource-constrained" activities.
- *Projects are developed to resolve a clear goal or set of goals.* There is no such thing as a project team with an ongoing, nonspecific purpose. Its goals, or **deliverables,** define the nature of the project and that of its team. Projects are designed to yield a tangible result, either as a new product or service. Whether the goal is to build a bridge, implement a new accounts receivable system, or win a presidential election, the goal must be specific and the project organized to achieve a stated aim.
- *Projects are customer focused.* Whether the project is responding to the needs of an internal organizational unit (e.g., accounting) or intended to exploit a market opportunity external to the organization, the underlying purpose of any project is to satisfy customer needs. In the past, this goal was sometimes overlooked. Projects were considered successful if they attained technical, budgetary, or scheduling goals. More and more, however, companies have realized that the primary goal of a project is customer satisfaction. If that goal is neglected, a firm runs the risk of "doing the wrong things well"—pursuing projects that may be done efficiently but that ignore customer needs or fail commercially.

General Project Characteristics

Using these definitional elements, we can create a sense of the key attributes that all projects share. These characteristics are not only useful for better understanding projects; they also offer the basis for seeing how project-based work differs from other activities most organizations undertake.

Projects represent a special type of undertaking by any organization. Not surprisingly, the challenges in performing them right are sometimes daunting. Nevertheless, given the manner in which business continues to evolve on a worldwide scale, becoming "project savvy" is no longer a luxury: It is rapidly becoming a necessity. Projects are characterized by the following properties:[11]

1. *Projects are ad hoc endeavors with a clear life cycle.*   Projects are nontraditional; they are activities that are initiated as needed, operate for a specified time period over a fairly well understood development cycle, and are then disbanded. They are temporary operations.

2. *Projects are building blocks in the design and execution of organizational strategies.*   As we will see in later chapters, projects allow organizations to implement companywide strategies. They are the principal means by which companies operationalize corporate-level objectives. In effect, projects are the vehicles for realizing company goals. For example, Intel's strategy for market penetration with ever newer, smaller, and faster computer chips is realized through its commitment to a steady stream of research and development projects that allows the company to continually explore the technological boundaries of electrical and computer engineering.

3. *Projects are responsible for the newest and most improved products, services, and organizational processes.*   Projects are tools for innovation. Because they complement (and often transform) traditional process-oriented activities, many companies rely on projects as vehicles for going beyond conventional activities. Projects are the stepping-stones by which we move forward.

4. *Projects provide a philosophy and strategy for the management of change.*   "Change" is an abstract concept until we establish the means by which we can make real alterations in the things we do and produce. Sometimes called the "building blocks of strategy," projects allow organizations to go beyond simple statements of intent and to achieve actual innovation. For example, whether it is Toyota's latest hybrid car or Apple's newest iPhone upgrade, successful organizations routinely ask for customer input and feedback to better understand their likes and dislikes. As the vehicle of change, the manner in which a company develops its projects has much to say about its ability to innovate and commitment to change.

5. *Project management entails crossing functional and organizational boundaries.*   Projects epitomize internal organizational collaboration by bringing together people from various functions across the company. A project aimed at new product development may require the combined work of engineering, finance, marketing, design, and so forth. Likewise, in the global business environment, many companies have crossed organizational boundaries by forming long-term partnerships with other firms in order to maximize opportunities while emphasizing efficiency and keeping a lid on costs. Projects are among the most common means of promoting collaboration, both across functions and across organizations.

6. *The traditional management functions of planning, organizing, motivation, directing, and control apply to project management.*   Project managers must be technically well versed, proficient at administrative functions, willing and able to assume leadership roles, and, above all, goal oriented: The project manager is the person most responsible for keeping track of the big picture. The nature of project management responsibilities should never be underestimated precisely because they are both diverse and critical to project success.

7. *The principal outcomes of a project are the satisfaction of customer requirements within the constraints of technical, cost, and schedule objectives.*   Projects are defined by their limitations. They have finite budgets, definite schedules, and carefully stated specifications for completion. For example, a term paper assignment in a college class might include details regarding form, length, number of primary and secondary sources to cite, and so forth. Likewise, in the Disney's Expedition Everest case example, the executive leading the change process established clear guidelines regarding performance expectations. All these constraints both limit and narrowly define the focus of the project and the options available to the project team. It is the very task of managing successful project development within such specific constraints that makes the field so challenging.

8. *Projects are terminated upon successful completion of performance objectives*—or earlier in their life cycle, if results no longer promise an operational or strategic advantage. As we have seen, projects differ

Source: DILBERT: © Scott Adams/Dist. by United Features Syndicate, Inc.

from conventional processes in that they are defined by limited life cycles. They are initiated, completed, and dissolved. As important alternatives to conventional organizational activities, they are sometimes called "temporary organizations."[12]

Projects, then, differ from better-known organizational activities, often involving repetitive processes. The traditional model of most firms views them as consistently performing a discrete set of activities. For example, a retail-clothing establishment buys, stocks, and sells clothes in a continuous cycle. A steel plant orders raw materials, makes steel, and ships finished products, again in a recurring cycle. The nature of these operations focuses our attention on a "process orientation," that is, the need to perform work as efficiently as possible in an ongoing manner. When its processes are this well understood, the organization seeks always to find better, more efficient ways of doing the same essential tasks. Projects, because they are discrete activities, violate the idea of repetition. They are temporary activities that operate outside formal channels. They may bring together a disparate collection of team members with different functional expertise. They function under conditions of uncertainty, and they usually have the effect of "shaking up" normal corporate activities. Because of their unique characteristics, they do not conform to common standards of operations; they do things differently and often reveal new and better ways of doing things. Table 1.1 offers some other distinctions between project-based work and these more traditional, process-based activities. Note a recurring theme: projects operate in radical ways that consistently violate the standard, process-based view of organizations.

Consider Apple's development of the iPod, a portable MP3 player that can be integrated with Apple's popular iTunes site to record and play music downloads. Apple, headed by its chairman, Steven Jobs, recognized the potential in the MP3 market, given the enormous popularity (and some would say, notoriety) of file-sharing and downloading music through the Internet. The company hoped to capitalize on the need for a customer-friendly MP3 player, while offering a legitimate alternative to illegal music downloading. Since its introduction, consumers have bought more than 170 million iPods and purchased more than 5 billion songs through Apple's iTunes online store. In fact, Apple's iTunes division is now the second largest music retailer in the United States, trailing only Wal-Mart.

TABLE 1.1 Differences Between Process and Project Management[13]

Process	Project
Repeat process or product	New process or product
Several objectives	One objective
Ongoing	One shot—limited life
People are homogenous	More heterogeneous
Well-established systems in place to integrate efforts	Systems must be created to integrate efforts
Greater certainty of performance, cost, schedule	Greater uncertainty of performance, cost, schedule
Part of line organization	Outside of line organization
Bastions of established practice	Violates established practice
Supports status quo	Upsets status quo

In an interview, Jobs acknowledged that Apple's business needed some shaking up, given the steady but unspectacular growth in sales of its flagship Macintosh personal computer, still holding approximately 9% of the overall PC market. The iPod, as a unique venture within Apple, became a billion-dollar business for the company in only its second year of existence. So popular has the iPod business become for Apple that the firm created a separate business unit, moving the product and its support staff away from the Mac group.

"Needless to say, iPod has become incredibly popular, even among people who aren't diehard Apple fanatics," industry analyst Paolo Pescatore told *NewsFactor,* noting that Apple recently introduced a smaller version of the product with great success. "In short, they have been very successful thus far, and I would guess they are looking at this realignment as a way to ensure that success will continue."[14]

Given the enthusiasm with which **project management** is being embraced by so many organizations, we should note that the same factors that make project management a unique undertaking are also among the main reasons why successful project management is so difficult. The track record of project management is by no means one of uninterrupted success, in part because many companies encounter deep-rooted resistance to the kinds of changes needed to accommodate a "project philosophy." Indeed, recent research into the success rates for projects offers some grim conclusions:

- A study of more than 300 large companies conducted by the consulting firm Peat Marwick found that software and/or hardware development projects fail at the rate of 65%. Of companies studied, 65% reported projects that went grossly over budget, fell behind schedule, did not perform as expected, or all of the above. Half of the managers responding indicated that these findings were considered "normal."[15]
- A study by the META Group found that "more that half of all (information technology) IT projects become runaways—overshooting their budgets and timetables while failing to deliver fully on their goals."[16]
- Applied Data Research surveys report that up to 75% of software projects are canceled.[17]
- According to the 2004 PriceWaterhouseCoopers Survey of 10,640 projects valued at $7.2 billion, across a broad range of industries, large and small, only 2.5% of global businesses achieve 100% project success and over 50% of global business projects fail. The Chaos Survey by The Standish Group reports similar findings. They say that the majority of all projects are either "challenged" (due to late delivery, being over-budget, or delivering less than required features), or "failed" and are canceled prior to completion or the product developed is never used. Researchers conclude that the average success rate of business-critical application development projects is 35%. Their statistics have remained remarkably steady since 1994.[18]
- The Special Inspector General for Iraq Reconstruction (SIGIR) reported that the Pentagon spent about $600 million on more than 1,200 Iraq reconstruction projects that were eventually cancelled, with 42% terminated due to mismanagement or shoddy construction.[19]

These findings underscore an important point: Although project management is becoming popular, it is not easy to assimilate into the conventional processes of most firms. For every firm discovering the benefits of projects, there are many more underestimating the problems involved in becoming "project savvy." These studies also point to a core truth about project management: We should not overestimate the benefits to be gained from project management while underestimating the commitment required to make it work. There are no magic bullets or quick fixes in the discipline. Like any other valuable activity, it requires preparation, knowledge, training, and commitment to basic principles. Organizations wanting to make use of project-based work must recognize, as Table 1.1 demonstrates, that its very strength often causes it to operate in direct contradiction to standard, process-oriented business practices.

1.2 WHY ARE PROJECTS IMPORTANT?

There are a number of reasons why projects and project management can be crucial in helping an organization achieve its strategic goals. David Cleland, a noted project management researcher, suggests that many of these reasons arise from the very pressures that organizations find themselves facing.[20]

1. ***Shortened product life cycles.***   The days when a company could offer a new product and depend upon years of competitive domination are gone. Increasingly, the life cycle of new products is measured in terms of months or even weeks, rather than years. One has only to look at new products in electronics

or computer hardware and software to observe this trend. Interestingly, we are seeing similar signs in traditional service sector firms, which have also recognized the need for agility in offering and upgrading new services at an increasingly rapid pace.

2. ***Narrow product launch windows.*** Another time-related issue concerns the nature of opportunity. Organizations are aware of the dangers of missing the optimum point at which to launch a new product and must take a proactive view toward the timing of product introductions. For example, while reaping the profits from the successful sale of Product A, smart firms are already plotting the best point at which to launch Product B, either as a product upgrade or a new offering. Because of fierce competition, these optimal launch opportunities are measured in terms of months. Miss your launch window, even by a matter of weeks, and you run the risk of rolling out an also-ran.

3. ***Increasingly complex and technical products.*** The world today is complex. Products are complicated, technically sophisticated, and difficult to produce efficiently. The public's appetite for "the next big thing" continues unabated and substantially unsatisfied. We want the new models of our consumer goods to be better, bigger (or smaller), faster, and more complex than the old ones. Firms constantly upgrade product and service lines to feed this demand. That causes multiple problems in design and production as we continually seek to push the technical limits. Further, in anticipating future demand, many firms embark on expensive programs of research and development while attempting to discern consumer tastes. The effect can be to erroneously create expensive and technically sophisticated projects that we assume the customer will want. For example, Rauma Corporation of Finland developed a state-of-the-art "loader" for the logging industry. Rauma's engineers loaded the product with the latest computerized gadgetry and technologies that gave the machine a space age feel. Unfortunately, the chief customer for the product worked in remote regions of Indonesia, with logistics problems that made servicing and repairing the loaders impractical. The machines, in the event of breakdowns, would require airlifting over 1,000 miles to service centers. Since its inception, sales of the logging machinery have been disappointing. The result was an expensive failure for Rauma and serves to illustrate an important point: Unless companies find a way to maintain control of the process, this "engineering for engineering's sake" mentality can quickly run out of control.[21]

4. ***Emergence of global markets.*** The past decade has seen the emergence of enormous new markets for almost every type of product and service. Former closed or socialist economies, such as Russia, China, and India, have added huge numbers of consumers and competitors to the global business arena. The increased globalization of the economy, coupled with enhanced methods for quickly interacting with customers and suppliers, has created a new set of challenges for business. These challenges also encompass unique opportunities for those firms that can quickly adjust to this new reality. In this global setting, project management techniques provide companies with the ability to link multiple business partners, respond quickly to market demand and supplier needs, while remaining agile enough to anticipate and respond to rapid shifts in consumer tastes. Using project management, successful organizations of the future will recognize and learn to rapidly exploit the prospects offered by a global business environment.

5. ***An economic period marked by low inflation.*** One of the key indicators of economic health is the fact that inflation has been kept under control. In most of the developed western economies, low inflation has helped to trigger a long period of economic expansion, while also helping provide the impetus for emerging economies, such as those in India and China, to expand rapidly. Unfortunately, low inflation also limits the ability of businesses to maintain profitability by passing along cost increases. Companies cannot continue to increase profit margins through simply raising prices for their products or services. Successful firms in the future will be those that enhance profits by streamlining internal processes—who save money by "doing it better" than their competition. As a tool designed to realize such goals as internal efficiency, project management is also a means to bolster profits.

These are just some of the more obvious challenges facing business today. The key point is that the forces giving rise to these challenges are not likely to abate in the near term. In order to meet them, companies as large and successful as General Electric, 3M, Nokia, Sony, Bechtel, and Microsoft have made project management a key aspect of their operating philosophies.

PROJECT PROFILE

Dubai—Land of Mega-Projects

If you were to award the prize for most unique building projects in the past decade, the winner might just be Dubai. Dubai, an emirate in the Persian Gulf, is a country of just under 4.5 million inhabitants and blessed with enormous reserves of oil, is one of the richest countries in the world. In the past two decades, the emirate has embarked on a massive construction program aimed at attracting tourists and residents from around the world. As a means to achieving this goal, Dubai is the center of some of the most innovative and eye-catching construction projects on earth.

A partial list of recent construction projects is impressive, including:

1. *Hydropolis*—The world's first underwater luxury resort brings new meaning to the "ocean-view room." Situated 66 feet *below* the surface of the Persian Gulf, it will include three elements: the land station, where guests will be welcomed, the connecting tunnel, which will transport people by train to the main area of the hotel, and the 220 suites within the submarine leisure complex. It is one of the largest contemporary construction projects in the world, covering an area of 260 hectares, about the size of London's Hyde Park. Reinforced by concrete and steel, its Plexiglas walls and bubble-shaped dome ceilings offer sights of fish and other sea creatures. It is scheduled in open in late 2009.
2. *The Palm Islands*—The three artificial islands that make up the Palm (the Palm Jumeirah, the Palm Jebel Ali, and the Palm Deira) are the world's biggest man-made islands. Each was built from a staggering 1 billion cubic meters of dredged sand and stone, taken from Dubai's sea bed and configured into individual islands and surrounding breakwaters. The complex will house a variety of tourist attractions, ranging from spas and diving sites to apartments and theaters. The entire complex is designed to collectively resemble a date palm tree when seen from the sky (see photo).
3. *The World*—Another artificial island project, the World is a group of more than 250 man-made islands designed to resemble the entire world when seen from the air. The islands, which range from 250,000 to 900,000 square feet, can be bought by individual developers or private owners—starting at $6.85 million. The only way to get to each island is by boat. The project incorporates two protective breakwaters to protect the islands from waves, consisting of one submerged reef (the outer breakwater) and an above-water structure (the inner breakwater).

FIGURE 1.2   **Aerial View of Dubai's "The Palms"**

4. ***Dubailand***—a fully functional city set up as a complex of seven theme parks, Dubailand includes more than 45 individual, multimillion-dollar projects. With 55 hotels and over 3 billion square feet, Dubailand will comprise a site that includes theme parks, centers of culture and art, science and planetariums, sports and sports academies, well-being and health, as well as shopping and retail. The venture is expected to attract 200,000 visitors daily and cost $20 billion. Many believe Dubailand is a long-term plan to phase out the city's dependence on oil revenues. Just one center, Dubailand's Sports City, will offer visitors a staggering variety of athletic venues, from elegant, gigantic stadia to state-of-the-art participatory parks for skateboarding, indoor rock climbing, and other activities. There will also be facilities for polo, car racing, golf, and extreme sports.

5. ***Burj Dubai***—The Burj Dubai will be the world's tallest building when it opens in 2009. The tip of the uppermost spire will be visible 60 miles away. Its shape is inspired by the desert flowers that often appear as decorative patterns in Islamic architecture, but it also has an engineering purpose: The swirl shape ensures that the mass of the structure lessens as it reaches the top, making the structure steadier. The building is expected to cost over $1 billion when completed and will be the centerpiece of the Burj Dubai complex and Dubai Mall, and it is expected to cost over $20 billion when completed in late 2009. The Dubai Mall, at more than 5 million square feet, is the largest shopping mall in the world. It houses 15 submalls, a skating rink, an aquarium, and the world's largest gold market.

This is only a partial list of many equally breathtaking ambitious projects. Indoor ski slopes, championship golf courses created out of the desert, the list goes on and on. Dubai's government cannot be faulted for the sheer breadth of its vision, aimed at using projects to transform the landscape of this small emirate into a unique center for tourism and travel in the world.[22]

Project management also serves as an excellent training ground for future senior executives in most organizations. One of the unique aspects of projects is their blend of technical and behavioral challenges. The technical side of project management requires managers to become skilled in project selection, budgeting and resource management, planning and scheduling, and tracking their projects. Each of these skills will be discussed in subsequent chapters. At the same time, however, project managers face the equally strong challenge of managing the behavioral, or "people side" of projects. Projects, being temporary endeavors, require project managers to bring together individuals from across the organization, quickly mold them into an effective team, manage conflict, provide leadership, and engage in negotiation and appropriate political behavior, all in the name of project success. Again, we will address these behavioral challenges in this text. One thing we know: Project managers who emphasize one challenge and ignore the other, whether they choose to focus on the technical or behavioral sides of project management, are not nearly as successful as those who seek to become experts at both. Why is project management such a useful training ground for senior executives? Because it provides the first true test of an individual's ability to master both the technical and human challenges that characterize effective leaders in business. Project managers, and their projects, create the kind of value that companies need to survive and prosper.

1.3 PROJECT LIFE CYCLES

Imagine receiving a term paper assignment in a college class. Our first step would be to develop a sense of the assignment itself—what the professor is looking for, how long the paper should be, the number of references required, stylistic expectations, and so forth. Once we have familiarized ourselves with the assignment, our next step will likely be to begin developing a plan for how we intend to proceed with the project in order to complete it by the date it is due. We make a rough guess as to how long the research will take, how much time will be needed for writing the first draft, proofing the paper, and completing the final draft, and use this information to begin creating some tentative milestones for the various components of the assignment. Next, we begin to execute our plan, doing the library or online research, creating an outline, writing a draft, and so forth. Our goal is to complete the assignment on time, doing the work to our best possible ability. Finally, after turning in the paper, we file or discard our reference materials, return any books to the library, breathe a sigh of relief, and wait for the grade.

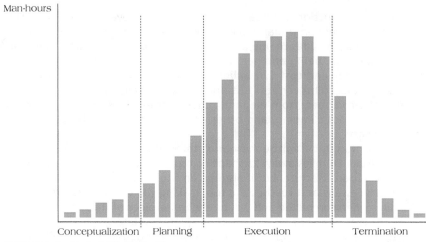

Man-hours

Conceptualization   Planning   Execution   Termination

FIGURE 1.3   Project Life Cycle Stages

Source: J. K. Pinto and P. Rouhaianen. 2002. *Building Customer-Based Project Organizations.* New York: Wiley. Reprinted with permission of John Wiley & Sons, Inc.

This example represents a simplified, but useful illustration of a project's life cycle. In this case, the project consisted of completing the term paper to the standards expected of the instructor in the time allowed. A **project life cycle** refers to the stages in a project's development. Life cycles are important because they demonstrate the logic that governs a project. They also help us develop our plans for carrying out the project. They help us decide, for example, when we should devote resources to the project, how we should evaluate its progress, and so forth. Consider the simplified model of the project life cycle shown in Figure 1.3, which divides the life cycle into four distinct phases: conceptualization, planning, execution, and termination.

- *Conceptualization* refers to the development of the initial goal and technical specifications for a project. The scope of the work is determined, necessary resources (people, money, physical plant) identified, and important organizational contributors or **stakeholders** signed on.
- *Planning* is the stage in which all detailed specifications, schematics, schedules, and other plans are developed. The individual pieces of the project, often called *work packages,* are broken down, individual assignments made, and the process for completion clearly delineated. For example, in planning our approach to complete the term paper, we determine all the necessary steps (research, drafts, editing, etc.) in the process.
- During *execution,* the actual "work" of the project is performed, the system developed, or the product created and fabricated. It is during the execution phase that the bulk of project team labor is performed. As Figure 1.3 shows, project costs ramp up rapidly during this stage.
- *Termination* occurs when the completed project is transferred to the customer, its resources reassigned, and the project formally closed out. As specific subactivities are completed, the project shrinks in scope and costs decline rapidly.

These stages are the waypoints at which the project team can evaluate both its performance and the project's overall status. Remember, however, that the life cycle is relevant only after the project has actually begun. The life cycle is signaled by the actual kickoff of project development, the development of plans and schedules, the performance of necessary work, and the completion of the project and reassignment of personnel. When we evaluate projects in terms of this life cycle model, we are given some clues regarding their subsequent resource requirements; that is, we begin to ask whether we have sufficient personnel, materials, or equipment to support the project. For example, when beginning to work on our term paper project, we may discover that it is necessary to purchase a PC or hire someone to help with researching the topic. Thus as we plan the project's life cycle, we also acquire important information regarding the resources that we will need. The life cycle model, then, serves the twofold function of

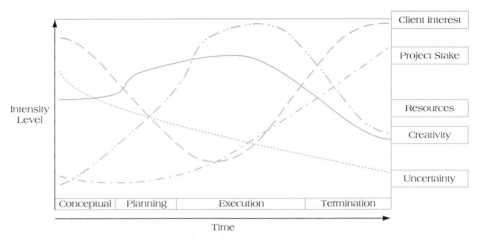

FIGURE 1.4 Project Life Cycles and Their Effects

Source: Victor Sohmen, "Project Termination: Why the Delay?" Paper presented at PMI Research Conference, July 2002, Seattle, WA.

project timing (schedule) and project requirements (resources), allowing team members to better focus on what and when resources are needed.

The project life cycle is also a useful means of visualizing the activities required and challenges to be faced during the life of a project. Figure 1.4 indicates some of these characteristics as they evolve during the course of completing a project.[23] As you can see, five components of a project may change over the course of its life cycle:

- **Client interest:**   The level of enthusiasm or concern expressed by the project's intended customer. **Clients** can be either internal to the organization or external.
- **Project stake:**   The amount of corporate investment in the project. The longer the life of the project, the greater the investment.
- **Resources:**   The commitment of financial, human, and technical resources over the life of the project.
- **Creativity:**   The degree of innovation required by the project, especially during certain development phases.
- **Uncertainty:**   The degree of risk associated with the project. Riskiness here reflects the number of unknowns, including technical challenges that the project is likely to face. Uncertainty is highest at the beginning because many challenges have yet to be identified, let alone addressed.

Each of these factors has its own dynamic. Client interest, for example, follows a "U-shaped" curve, reflecting initial enthusiasm, lower levels of interest during development phases, and renewed interest as the project nears completion. Project stake increases dramatically as the project moves forward because an increasing commitment of resources is needed to support ongoing activities. Creativity, often viewed as innovative thought or applying a unique perspective, is high at the beginning of a project, as the team and the project's client begin developing a shared vision of the project. As the project moves forward and uncertainty remains high, creativity also continues to be an important feature. In fact, it is not until the project is well into its execution phase, with defined goals, that creativity becomes less important. To return to our example of the term paper project, in many cases, the "creativity" needed to visualize a unique or valuable approach to developing the project is needed early, as we identify our goals and plan the process of achieving them. Once identified, the execution phase, or writing the term paper, places less emphasis on creativity per se and more on the concrete steps needed to complete the project assignment. The information simplified in Figure 1.4 is useful for developing a sense of the competing issues and challenges that a project team is likely to face over the life cycle of a project. Over time, while certain characteristics (creativity, resources, and uncertainty) begin to decrease, other elements (client interest and project stake) gain in importance. Balancing the requirements of these elements across the project life cycle is just one of the many demands placed upon a project team.

PROJECT MANAGERS IN PRACTICE

Christy Rutkowski, Regency Construction Services

"My major satisfaction is being a part of an awesome creation process. Seeing the drawings of something and then watching it going together really makes you feel like a little kid in awe. I also love working with so many different people for a common goal. In construction every day is different. Every day brings on new challenges, yet new accomplishments."

Christy A. Rutkowski is a Project Engineer for Regency Construction Services, working in Ohio. She has been involved in construction management since 2002 and with Regency since 2005. For the past seven years, she has been working on the construction and renovations of schools: elementary, middle, high and career centers with money made available through state funding in Ohio. Recently, she started working on the construction of a $150 million hospital. Her role in these projects involves numerous activities, including working with architects and owners to ensure the building is being designed to meet state regulations. She must then coordinate all departments in her own company in order to ensure the building is being designed within budget and on schedule. Finally, Christy is responsible for getting the project out to bid and working with contractors to ensure their knowledge of the project, answer any questions, coordinate any questions/answers with the architect, compose and post any addendums. Once bids are received she coordinates with legal counsel to compose contracts and kick off construction.

"As a project engineer—I am in the field full time working with the field staff and other contractors from ground breaking to ribbon cutting—I process change orders, pay applications, requests for information and submittals. I review each to ensure they comply with the drawings and specifications; change orders are valid and the cost is reasonable, etc."

"Currently I am working on a hospital for University Hospitals systems in Cleveland. The project is made up of a medical office building, hospital and central energy plant. The hospital is a $150 million, 200 bed facility that will serve many communities. The duration of this current project is three years. The staff managing the project consists of six superintendents, four project engineers, a manager, and a project executive. There are over 30 different contractors working on the job."

When asked about the challenges of her job, Christy observes, "Something that was initially challenging was learning the different aspects of construction. Learning how each component goes together comes from experience and studying the drawings. Also, as a woman in the construction field, it is a challenge to earn respect. It is extremely rewarding to be depended upon as part of the team and break through glass ceilings. In construction there are a lot of 'old school' perspectives on things and while it has been an uphill battle, it is rewarding to have the same people who initially wanted nothing to do with me (being a young woman) to come to depend on me to get the job done. One thing I learned for sure: you need really thick skin and a strong backbone, but that makes your accomplishments that much sweeter."

FIGURE 1.5   Christy Rutkowski, Regency Construction Services

1.4 DETERMINANTS OF PROJECT SUCCESS

Definitions of successful projects can be surprisingly elusive.[24] How do we know when a project is successful? When it is profitable? If it comes in on budget? On time? When the developed product works or sells? When we achieve our long-term payback goals? Generally speaking, any definition of **project success** *must* take into consideration the elements that define the very nature of a project: that is, time (schedule adherence), budget, functionality/quality, and customer satisfaction. At one time, managers normally applied three criteria of project success:

- **Time.**   Projects are constrained by a specified time frame during which they must be completed. They are not supposed to continue indefinitely. Thus the first constraint that governs project management involves the basic requirement: the project should come in on or before its established schedule.
- **Cost.**   A second key constraint for all projects is a limited budget. Projects must meet budgeted allowances in order to use resources as efficiently as possible. Companies do not write blank checks and hope for the best. Thus the second limit on a project raises the question: Was the project completed within budget guidelines?
- **Performance.**   All projects are developed in order to adhere to some initially determined technical specifications. We know before we begin what the project is supposed to do or how the final product is supposed to operate. Measuring performance, then, means determining whether the finished product operates according to specifications. The project's clients naturally expect that the project being developed on their behalf will work as expected. Applying this third criterion is often referred to as conducting a "quality" check.

This so-called **triple constraint** was once the standard by which project performance was routinely assessed. Today, a fourth criterion has been added to these three (see Figure 1.6):

- **Client acceptance.**   The principle of client acceptance argues that projects are developed with customers, or clients, in mind, and their purpose is to satisfy customers' needs. If client acceptance is a key variable, then we must also ask whether the completed project is acceptable to the customer for whom it was intended. Companies that evaluate project success strictly according to the original "triple constraint" may fail to apply the most important test of all: the client's satisfaction with the completed project.

We can also think of the criteria for project success in terms of "internal" vs. "external" conditions. When project management was practiced primarily by construction and other heavy industries, its chief value was in maintaining internal organizational control over expenditures of money and time. The traditional triple constraint made perfect sense. It focused internally, on efficiency and productivity measures. It provided a quantifiable measure of personnel evaluation, and it allowed accountants to control expenses.

More recently, however, the traditional triple constraint has come under increasing criticism as a measure of project success. The final product, for example, could be a failure, but if it has been delivered in time and on budget and satisfies its original specifications (however flawed), the project itself could still be

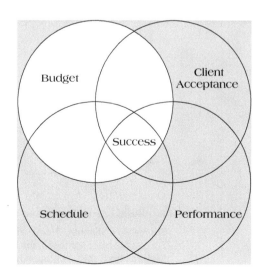

FIGURE 1.6 **The New Quadruple Constraint**

declared a success. Adding the external criterion of client acceptance corrects such obvious shortcomings in the assessment process. First, it refocuses corporate attention outside the organization, toward the customer, who will probably be dissatisfied with a failed or flawed final product. Likewise, it recognizes that the final arbiter of project success is not the firm's accountants, but rather the marketplace. A project is successful only to the extent that it benefits the client who commissioned it. Finally, the criterion of client acceptance requires project managers and teams to create an atmosphere of openness and communication throughout the development of the project.

Consider one recent example. The automaker Volvo has been motivated to increase its visibility and attractiveness to female customers, a market segment that has become significantly stronger over the years. The company's market research showed that women want everything in a car that men want, "plus a lot more that male car buyers never thought to ask for," according to Hans-Olov Olsson, the former president and CEO of Volvo. In fact, Volvo discovered, in Olsson's words, "If you meet women's expectations, you exceed those for men." Volvo's solution was to allow hundreds of its female employees, including an all-female design and engineering staff, to develop a new-generation concept car. The group studied a variety of vehicle aspects, including ergonomics, styling, storage, and maintenance, keeping in mind the common theme: What do women want? Code-named the YCC, the car is designed to be nearly maintenance free, with an efficient gas-electric hybrid engine, sporty styling, and roomy storage. Volvo's efforts in developing the YCC project demonstrate a commitment to client acceptance and satisfaction as a key motivator of its project management process, supplanting the traditional triple constraint model for project success.[25]

An additional approach to project assessment argues that another factor must always be taken into consideration: the promise that the delivered product can generate future opportunities, whether commercial or technical, for the organization.[26] In other words, it is not enough to assess a project according to its immediate success. We must also evaluate it in terms of its commercial success as well as its potential for generating new business and new opportunities. Figure 1.7 illustrates this scheme, which proposes four relevant dimensions of success:

- *Project efficiency:*   Meeting budget and schedule expectations.
- *Impact on the customer:*   Meeting technical specifications, addressing customer needs, and creating a project that satisfies the client's needs.
- *Business success:*   Determining whether the project achieved significant commercial success.
- *Future potential:*   Determining whether the project opened new markets or new product lines or helped to develop new technology.

This approach challenges the conventional triple constraint principle for assessing project success. Corporations expect projects not only to be run efficiently (at the least) but to be developed to meet customer

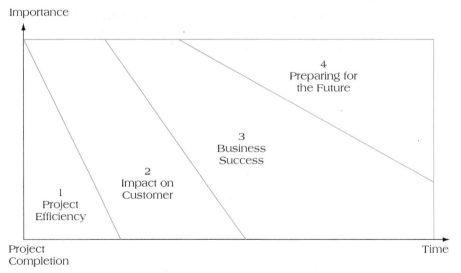

FIGURE 1.7 **Four Dimensions of Project Success Importance**

> ## BOX 1.2
>
> ## PROJECT MANAGEMENT RESEARCH IN BRIEF
>
> ### Assessing Information Technology (IT) Project Success
>
> As we noted earlier in this chapter, IT projects have a notoriously checkered history when it comes to successful implementation. Part of the problem has been an inability to define the characteristics of a successful IT project in concrete terms. The criteria for IT project success are often quite vague, and without clear guidelines for project success, it is hardly any wonder that so many of these projects do not live up to predevelopment expectations. In 1992 and again in 2003, two researchers, W. DeLone and E. McLean, analyzed several previous studies of IT projects to identify the key indicators of success. Their findings, synthesized from previous research, suggest that, at the very least, IT projects should be evaluated according to six criteria:
>
> - *System quality.* The project team supplying the system must be able to assure the client that the implemented system will perform as intended. All systems should satisfy certain criteria: They should, for example, be easy to use, and they should supply quality information.
> - *Information quality.* The information generated by the implemented IT must be the information required by users and be of sufficient quality that it is "actionable": In other words, generated information should not require additional efforts to sift or sort the data. System users can perceive quality in the information they generate.
> - *Use.* Once installed, the IT system must be used. Obviously, the reason for any IT system is its usefulness as a problem-solving, decision-aiding, and networking mechanism. The criterion of "use" assesses the actual utility of a system by determining the degree to which, once implemented, it is used by the customer.
> - *User satisfaction.* Once the IT system is complete, the project team must determine user satisfaction. One of the thorniest issues in assessing IT project success has to do with making an accurate determination of user satisfaction with the system. Yet, because the user is the client and is ultimately the arbiter of whether or not the project was effective, it is vital that we attain some measure of the client's satisfaction with the system and its output.
> - *Individual impact.* All systems should be easy to use and should supply quality information. But beyond satisfying these needs, is there a specific criterion for determining the usefulness of a system to the client who commissioned it? Is decision making faster or more accurate? Is information more retrievable, more affordable, or more easily assimilated? In short, does the system benefit users in the ways that are most important to those users?
> - *Organizational impact.* Finally, the supplier of the system must be able to determine whether it has a positive impact throughout the client organization. Is there, for example, a collective or synergistic effect on the client corporation? Is there a sense of good feeling, or are there financial or operational metrics that demonstrate the effectiveness or quality of the system?
>
> DeLone and McLean's work provides an important framework for establishing a sense of IT project success. Companies that are designing and implementing IT systems must pay early attention to each of these criteria and take necessary steps to ensure that the systems that they deliver satisfy them.[27]

needs, achieve commercial success, and serve as conduits to new business opportunities. Even in the case of a purely internal project (for example, updating the software for a firm's order-entry system), project teams need to focus on customer needs as well as to assess potential commercial or technical opportunities arising from their efforts.

A final model, offered recently, also argues against the triple-constraint model as a measure of project success. According to Atkinson,[28] all groups that are affected by a project (stakeholders) should have a hand in assessing its success. The context and type of a project may also be relevant in specifying the criteria that will most clearly define its success or failure. Table 1.2 shows the Atkinson model, which views the traditional "iron triangle" of cost, quality, and time as merely one set of components in a comprehensive set of measures. Of course, the means by which a project is to be measured should be decided before the project is undertaken. A corporate axiom, "What gets measured, gets managed," suggests that when teams understand the standards to which a project is being held, they will place more appropriate emphasis on project performance. Consider, for example, an information system setting. If the criteria of success are improved operating efficiency and satisfied users, and if quality is clearly identified as a key benefit of the finished product, the team will focus its efforts more strongly on these particular aspects of the project.

TABLE 1.2 Understanding Success Criteria

Iron Triangle	Information System	Benefits (Organization)	Benefits (Stakeholders)
Cost	Maintainability	Improved efficiency	Satisfied users
Quality	Reliability	Improved effectiveness	Social and environmental impact
Time	Validity	Increased profits	
	Information quality	Strategic goals	Personal development
	Use	Organization learning	Professional learning, contractors' profits
		Reduced waste	Capital suppliers, content
			Project team, economic impact to surrounding community

1.5 DEVELOPING PROJECT MANAGEMENT MATURITY

With the tremendous increase in project management practices among global organizations, a recent phenomenon has been the rise of project maturity models for project management organizations. **Project management maturity models** are used to allow organizations to benchmark the best practices of successful project management firms. Project management maturity models recognize that different organizations are currently at different levels of sophistication in their best practices for managing projects. For example, it would be reasonable to expect an organization such as Boeing (aircraft and defense systems) or Fluor-Daniel (industrial construction) to be much more advanced in how they manage projects, given their lengthy history of project initiatives, than a company that has only recently developed an emphasis on project-based work.

The purpose of **benchmarking** is to systematically manage the process improvements of project delivery by a single organization over a period of time.[29] Because there are many diverse dimensions of project management practice, it is common for a new organization just starting to introduce project management to its operations to ask, "Where do we start?" That is, which of the multiple project management processes should we investigate, model, and apply to our organization? Maturity models provide the necessary framework to first, analyze and critically evaluate current practices as they pertain to managing projects; second, compare those practices against those of chief competitors or some general industry standard; and third, define a systematic route for improving these practices.

If we accept the fact that the development of better project management practices is an evolutionary process, involving not a sudden leap to top performance but rather a systematic commitment to continuous improvement, maturity models offer the template for defining and then achieving such a progressive improvement.[30] As a result, most effective project maturity models chart both a set of standards that are currently accepted as state-of-the-art as well as a process for achieving significant movement toward these benchmarks. Figure 1.8 illustrates one approach to defining current project management practices a firm is using.[31] It employs a "spider web" methodology in which a set of significant project management practices have first been identified for organizations within a specific industry. In this example, a firm may identify eight components of project management practice that are key for their success, based on an analysis of their own needs as well as through benchmarking against competing firms in their industry. Note that each of the rings in the diagram represents a critical evaluation of the manner in which the organization matches up with industry standards. Suppose we assigned the following meanings to the different ratings:

Ring Level	Meaning
0	Not defined or poor
1	Defined but substandard
2	Standardized
3	Industry leader or cutting edge

Following this example, we may decide that in terms of project team personnel development or project control systems, our practices are poor relative to other competitors and rate those skills as 0. On the other hand, perhaps

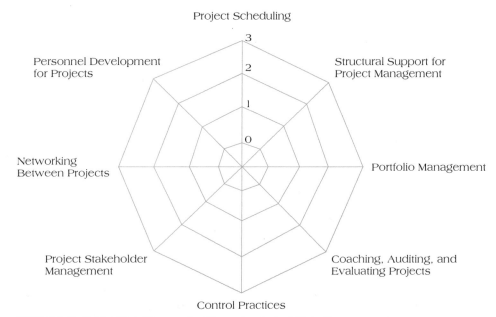

FIGURE 1.8 **Spider Web Diagram for Measuring Project Maturity**

Source: R. Gareis, "Competencies in the Project-Oriented Organization," in D. Slevin, D. Cleland, and J. Pinto, *The Frontiers of Project Management Research,* 213–224, figure on page 216. Newtown Square, PA: Project Management Institute. Copyright and all rights reserved. Material from this publication has been reproduced with the permission of PMI.

our scheduling processes are top notch, enabling us to rate them as a 3. Figure 1.9 shows an example of the same spider web diagram with our relative skill levels defined and assigned across the eight key elements of project management we have defined. This exercise helps us to form the basis for where we currently are in terms of project management sophistication, a key stage in any maturity model in which we seek to move to a higher level.

Once we have established a sense of our present project management abilities, as well as our shortcomings, the next step in the maturity model process is to begin charting a step-by-step, incremental path to our desired goal. Table 1.3 highlights some of the more common project maturity models and the interim levels

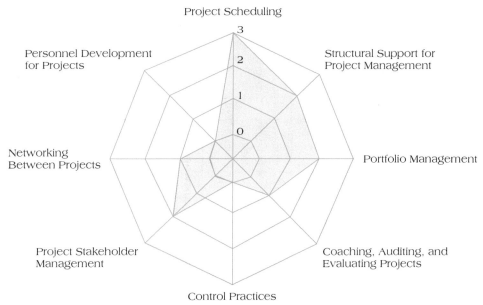

FIGURE 1.9 **Spider Web Diagram with Embedded Organizational Evaluation**

Source: R. Gareis, "Competencies in the Project-Oriented Organization," in D. Slevin, D. Cleland, and J. Pinto, *The Frontiers of Project Management Research,* 213–224, figure on page 216. Newtown Square, PA: Project Management Institute. Copyright and all rights reserved. Material from this publication has been reproduced with the permission of PMI.

TABLE 1.3 A Comparison of Project Maturity Models and Incremental Stages

Center for Business Practices

Level 1: Initial Process	Level 2: Structure, Process, and Standards	Level 3: Institutionalized Project Management	Level 4: Managed	Level 5: Optimizing
• Ad hoc process • Management awareness	• Basic processes, not standard on all projects • Management supports use • Estimates, schedules based on expert knowledge	• All project processes are repeatable • Estimates, schedules based on industry standards	• Project management practices integrated with corporate processes • Solid analysis of project performance • Estimates, schedules based on corporate specifics	• Processes to measure project efficiency • Processes in place to improve project performance • Company focuses on continuous improvement

Kerzner's Project Management Maturity Model

Level 1: Common Language	Level 2: Common Processes	Level 3: Singular Methodology	Level 4: Benchmarking	Level 5: Continuous Improvement
• Sporadic use of project management • Small pockets of interest in the firm • No investment in PM training	• Tangible benefits made apparent • PM support throughout the firm • Development of a PM curriculum	• Integrated processes • Cultural and management support • Financial benefit from PM training	• Analysis and evaluation of practices • Project office established	• Lessons learned, files created • Knowledge transfer between teams • Mentorship program

ESI International's Project Framework

Level 1: Ad Hoc	Level 2: Consistent	Level 3: Integrated	Level 4: Comprehensive	Level 5: Optimizing
• Processes ill-defined because they are applied individually • Little support by organization	• Organization is well intentioned in its methods • No project control processes or lessons learned	• Processes are tailored to enhance all PM aspects • Common use and understanding of methods across the firm	• PM fully implemented across the firm • Information is used to evaluate processes and reduce variation • Advanced PM tools and techniques are developed	• Continual effort to improve and innovate project capability • Common failures are eliminated

SEI's Capability Maturity Model Integration

Level 1: Initial	Level 2: Managed	Level 3: Defined	Level 4: Quantitative Management	Level 5: Optimizing
• Ad hoc, chaotic processes	• Requirements management, project planning, and control occur • Process quality assurance occurs • Configuration management is used	• Requirements development and product integration occur • Verification and validation of processes • Risk management is emphasized	• Process performance is gauged • Quantitative PM highlighted	• Innovation and deployment accentuated • Causal analysis and resolution occur

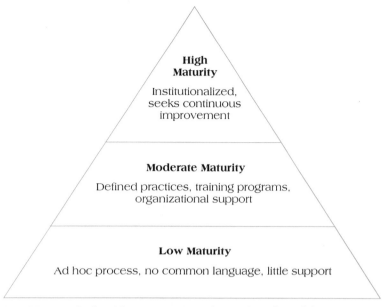

FIGURE 1.10 **Project Management Maturity—A Generic Model**

they have identified en route to the highest degree of organization-wide project expertise. Several of these models were developed by private project management consultancies or professional project organizations.

It is interesting to compare and contrast the four maturity models highlighted in Table 1.3. These maturity models are examples from among the most well known in the field, including Carnegie Mellon University's Software Engineering Institute's (SEI) Capability Maturity Model, Harold Kerzner's Maturity Model, ESI International's Project Framework, and the maturity model developed by the Center for Business Practices.[32] Illustrating these dimensions in pyramid form, we can see from Figure 1.10 the progression toward project management maturity. Despite some differences in terminology, there is a clear sense of pattern among each of these models. They typically start with the assumption that project management practices within a firm are not planned and are not collectively employed; in fact, there is likely no common language or methods for undertaking project management. As the firm grows in project maturity, it begins to adopt common practices, starts programs to train cadres of project management professionals, establishes procedures and processes for initiating and controlling its projects, and so forth. Finally, by the last stage, not only is the organization "project-savvy," but it also has progressed beyond simply applying project management to its processes and is now actively exploring ways to continuously improve its project management techniques and procedures. It is during the final stage that the organization can be truly considered "project mature"; it has internalized all necessary project management principles and it is actively seeking to move beyond these in innovative ways.

Project maturity models have become very useful in recent years precisely because they reflect the growing interest in project management while highlighting one of the recurring problems: the lack of clear direction for companies in adopting, adapting, and improving these processes for optimal use. The key feature of these models is the important recognition that change typically does not occur abruptly; that is, companies that desire to become skilled in their project management approaches simply cannot progress in immediate steps from a lack of project management understanding to optimal project practices. Instead, the maturity models note that "maturity" is an ongoing process, based on continuous improvement through identifiable incremental steps. Once we have an accurate picture of where we fit into the maturity picture, we can begin to determine a reasonable course of progression to our desired level. In this manner, any organization, no matter how initially unskilled in project management, can begin to chart a course toward the type of project organization it hopes to become.

1.6 PROJECT ELEMENTS AND TEXT ORGANIZATION

This text was written to provide a holistic, managerial-based approach to project management. The text is holistic in that it weaves together the wide variety of duties, responsibilities, and knowledge that successful project managers must acquire. Project management is a comprehensive and exciting undertaking. It requires

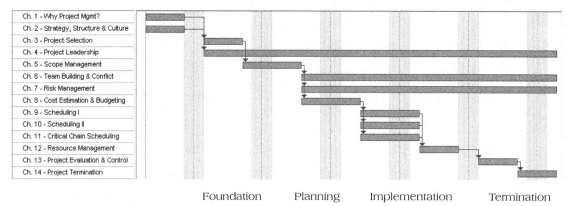

Ch. 1 - Why Project Mgmt?
Ch. 2 - Strategy, Structure & Culture
Ch. 3 - Project Selection
Ch. 4 - Project Leadership
Ch. 5 - Scope Management
Ch. 6 - Team Building & Conflict
Ch. 7 - Risk Management
Ch. 8 - Cost Estimation & Budgeting
Ch. 9 - Scheduling I
Ch. 10 - Scheduling II
Ch. 11 - Critical Chain Scheduling
Ch. 12 - Resource Management
Ch. 13 - Project Evaluation & Control
Ch. 14 - Project Termination

Foundation   Planning   Implementation   Termination

FIGURE 1.11 **Organization of Text**

us to understand aspects of management science in building schedules, assigning resources, monitoring and controlling our projects, and so forth. At the same time, successful project managers also must integrate fundamental issues of behavioral science, involving knowledge of human beings, leadership practices, motivation and team development, conflict resolution, and negotiation skills. Truly, a "science-heavy" approach to this subject will make us no more successful in our future project management responsibilities than will a focus that retains an exclusively "people-based" outlook. Project management is an exciting and challenging blend of the science and art of management.

Figure 1.11 offers a model for the organization of this text. The figure is a Gantt chart, a project scheduling and control device that we will become more familiar with in Chapter 10. For now, however, we can apply it to the structure of this book by focusing on some of its simpler features. First, note that all chapters in the book are listed down the left-hand column. Across the bottom and running from left to right is a simple time line that illustrates the point at which each of the chapters' topics will be introduced. For simplicity's sake, I have divided the X-axis time line into four distinct project phases that roughly follow the project life cycle discussed earlier in this chapter: (1) Foundation, (2) Planning, (3) Implementation, and (4) Termination. Notice how some of the topics we will cover are particularly relevant only during certain phases of the project while others, such as project leadership, are significant across much of the project's life cycle. Among the benefits of setting up the text to follow this sequence are that, first, it shows the importance of blending the human-based topics (leadership and team building) directly with the more analytical or scientific elements of project management. We cannot compartmentalize our approach to project management as either exclusively technical or behavioral; the two are opposite sides of the same coin and must be appreciated jointly. Second, the structure provides a simple logic for ordering the chapters and the stage of the project at which we are most likely to concern ourselves with these topics. Some concepts, as illustrated by the figure, are more immediately concerned with project planning while others become critical at later phases in the project. Appreciating the elements of project management *and their proper sequencing* is an important learning guide. Finally, the figure offers an intuitively appealing method for visually highlighting the structure and flow we will follow across the topics in the text.

The foundation stage helps us with our fundamental understanding of what projects are and how they are typically managed in modern organizations. As part of that understanding, we must necessarily focus on the organizational setting within which projects are created, selected, and developed. Some of the critical issues that can affect the manner in which projects are successfully implemented are the contextual issues of a firm's strategy, structure, and culture (Chapter 2). Either these elements are set up to support project-based work or they are not. In the former case, it is far easier to run projects and achieve positive results for the organization. As a result, it is extremely helpful for us to clearly understand the role that organizational setting, or context, plays in project management.

In Chapter 3 we explore the process of project screening and selection. The manner in which a firm selects the projects it chooses to undertake is often critical to its chances of successful development and commercial profitability. Chapter 4 introduces the challenges of project management from the perspective of the project leader. Project management is an extremely "leader-intensive" undertaking: The project manager is the focal point of the project, often functioning as a miniature CEO. The more they understand about project leadership and the skills required by effective project managers, the better companies can begin training project managers within their own ranks.

The second phase is related to the up-front issues of project planning. Once a decision to proceed has been made, the organization must first select a suitable project manager to oversee the development process. Immediately, this project manager is faced with a number of responsibilities, including:

1. *Selecting a team*—Team building and conflict management are the first challenges that project managers face.
2. *Developing project objectives and a plan for execution*—Identifying project requirements and a logical plan to develop the project are crucial.
3. *Performing risk management activities*—Projects are not developed without a clear sense of the risks involved in their planning and implementation.
4. *Cost estimating and budgeting*—Because projects are resource-constrained activities, careful budgeting and cost estimation are critical.
5. *Scheduling*—The heart of project planning revolves around the process of creating clear, aggressive, yet reasonable schedules that chart the most efficient course to project completion.
6. *Managing resources*—The final step in project planning is the careful management of project resources, including project team personnel, to most efficiently perform tasks.

Chapter 5, which discusses project scope management, examines the key features in the overall plan. "Project scope management" is something of an umbrella term under which we consider a number of elements in the overall project planning process. This chapter elaborates the variety of planning techniques and steps for getting a project off on the right foot. Chapter 6 addresses some of the behavioral challenges project managers face in terms of effective team building and conflict management. Chapter 6 looks at another key component of effective human resource management: the need to create and maintain high-performance teams. Effectively building and nurturing team members—often people from very different backgrounds—is a constant challenge and one that requires serious consideration. Conflict occurs on a number of levels, not just among team members, but between the team and project stakeholders, including top management and customers. This chapter will identify some of the principal causes of conflict and explain various methods for resolving it. Chapter 7 deals with project risk management. In recent years, this area of project management has become increasingly important to companies that want to ensure, as far as possible, that project selection choices are appropriate, that all the risks and downside potential have been considered, and that, where appropriate, contingency plans have been developed. Chapter 8 covers budgeting and cost estimation. Because project managers and teams are held to both standards of performance and standards of cost control, it is important to understand the key features of cost estimation and budgeting. Chapters 9 and 10 focus on scheduling methodologies, which are a key feature of project management. These chapters offer an in-depth analysis of various project-scheduling tools, discuss critical software for project scheduling, and explain some recent breakthroughs in project scheduling. Chapter 11 covers a recent development in project scheduling, the development and application of critical chain project scheduling. Chapter 12 considers the challenges of resource allocation. Once various project activities have been identified, we must make sure they work by allocating the resources needed to support them.

The third process in project management, *implementation,* is most easily understood as the stage in which the actual "work" of the project is being performed. For example, engineers and other technical experts determine the series of tasks necessary to complete the overall project, including their individual task responsibilities, and each of the tasks is actively managed by the manager and team to ensure that there are no significant delays that can cause the project to exceed its schedule. Chapter 13 addresses the project challenges of control and evaluation. During the implementation phase, a considerable amount of ambiguity regarding the status of the project is possible, unless specific, practical steps are taken to establish a clear method for tracking and controlling the project.

Finally, the processes of project termination reflect the fact that a project is a unique organizational endeavor, marked by a specified beginning and ending. The process of closing down a project, either due to the need to "kill" it because it is no longer viable or through the steps of a planned termination, offers its own set of challenges. A number of procedures have been developed to make this process as smooth and logical as possible. Chapter 14 discusses the elements in project *close-out*—the phase in which the project is concluded and resources (both monetary and human) are reassigned.

This book was written to help create a new generation of effective project managers. By exploring the various roles of project managers and addressing the challenges and opportunities they constantly face, we will offer a comprehensive and integrative approach to better understanding the task of project management—one that explores the full range of strategic, technical, and behavioral challenges and duties for project managers.

This text also includes, at the end of relevant chapters, a series of activities designed to help students develop comprehensive project plans. It is absolutely essential that persons completing a course in project management carry away with them practical knowledge about the steps involved in creating a project, planning its development, and overseeing its work. Future managers need to develop the skills to convert the theories of project management to the successful practice of the craft. With this goal in mind, the text contains a series of exercises designed to help professors and students construct overall project plans. Activities involve the development, from beginning to end, of a project plan, including narrative, risk analysis, work breakdown structure, activity estimation and network diagramming, resource leveling and project budgeting, and so forth. In order to add a sense of realism to the process, later chapters in the book also include a series of hypothetical problems. By the end of the course, students should have created a comprehensive project document that details the necessary steps in converting project plans into practical accomplishments.

As a template for providing examples, the text employs a hypothetical company called ABCups Inc., which is about to initiate an important project. Chapter-ending activities, including exercises in scheduling, budgeting, risk management, and so forth, will often include examples created from the ABCups project for students to use as a model for their own work. In this way, they will be presented both with a challenge and with an example for generating their own deliverables as they progressively build their project plans.

An additional feature of this text is the linkage between concepts that are discussed throughout and the Project Management Body of Knowledge (PMBoK), which was developed by the Project Management Institute (PMI). As the world's leading professional organization for project management, PMI has been in the forefront of efforts to standardize project management practices and codify the necessary skills to be successful in our field. The PMBoK identifies nine knowledge areas of project management skills and activities that all practitioners need to master in order to become fully trained in their profession. These knowledge areas are shown in Figure 1.12 and encompass a broad overview of the component processes for project management. While it is not my intention to create a text to serve as a primer for taking a professional certification exam, it is important for us to recognize that the skills we develop through reading this work are directly applicable to the professional project management knowledge areas.

Students will find several direct links to the PMBoK in this text. First, the key terminology and their definitions are intended to follow the PMBoK glossary (included as an appendix at the end of the text). Second, chapter introductions will also highlight references to the PMBoK as we address them in turn. We can see how each chapter adds not only to our knowledge of project management but also directly links to

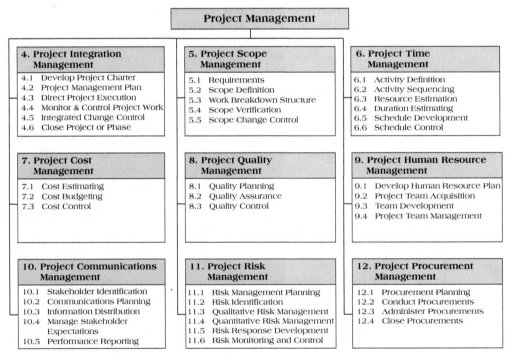

FIGURE 1.12 **Overview of the Project Management Institute's PMBoK Knowledge Areas**

Source: Project Management Institute. 2008. *A Guide to the Project Management Body of Knowledge (PMBoK Guide), Fourth Edition.* Project Management Institute, Inc. Copyright and all rights reserved. Material from this publication has been reproduced with the permission of PMI.

elements within the PMBoK. Finally, many end-of-chapter exercises and Internet references will require direct interaction with PMI through its Web site.

As an additional link to the Project Management Institute and the PMBoK, this text will include sample practice questions at the end of relevant chapters to allow students to test their in-depth knowledge of aspects of the PMBoK. Nearly 20 years ago, PMI instituted its Project Management Professional (PMP) certification as a means of awarding those with an expert knowledge of project management practice. The PMP certification is the highest professional designation for project management expertise in the world and requires in-depth knowledge in all nine areas of the PMBoK. The inclusion of questions at the end of the relevant chapters offers students a way to assess how well they have learned the important course topics, the nature of PMP certification exam questions, and to point to areas that may require additional study in order to master this material.

This text offers an opportunity for students to begin mastering a new craft—a set of skills that is becoming increasingly valued in contemporary corporations around the world. Project managers represent the new corporate elite: a corps of skilled individuals who routinely make order out of chaos, improving a firm's bottom line and burnishing their own value in the process. With these goals in mind, let us begin.

Summary

1. **Understand why project management is becoming such a powerful and popular practice in business today.** Project management offers organizations a number of practical competitive advantages, including the ability to be both effective in the marketplace and efficient with the use of organizational resources, and the ability to achieve technological breakthroughs, to streamline new-product development, and to manage the challenges arising from the business environment.

2. **Recognize the basic properties of projects, including their definition.** Projects are defined as temporary endeavors undertaken to create a unique product or service. Among their key properties are that projects are complex, one-time processes; projects are limited by budget, schedule, and resources; they are developed to resolve a clear goal or set of goals; and they are customer focused.

3. **Understand why effective project management is such a challenge.** Projects operate outside of normal organizational processes, typified by the work done by functional organizational units. Because they are unique, they require a different mind-set; one that is temporary, aimed at achieving a clear goal, within a limited time frame. Projects are ad hoc endeavors with a clear life cycle. They are employed as the building blocks in the design and execution of organizational strategies, and they provide a philosophy and a strategy for the management of change. Other reasons why they are a challenge include the fact that project management requires the crossing of functional and organizational boundaries while trying to satisfy the multiple constraints of time, budget, functionality, and customer satisfaction.

4. **Differentiate between project management practices and more traditional, process-oriented business functions.** Projects involve new process or product ideas, typically with one objective or a limited set of objectives. They are one-shot activities with a defined beginning and end, employing a heterogeneous group of organizational members as the project team. They operate under circumstances of change and uncertainty, outside of normal organizational channels, and are intended to upset the status quo and violate established practice, if need be, in order to achieve project goals. Process-oriented functions adhere more closely to rigid organizational rules, channels of communication, and procedures. The people within the functional departments are homogenous, engaged in ongoing activities, with well-established systems and procedures. They represent bastions of established practice designed to reinforce the organization's status quo.

5. **Recognize the key motivators that are pushing companies to adopt project management practices.** Among the key motivators in pushing organizations to adopt project management are (1) shortened product life cycles, (2) narrow product launch windows, (3) increasingly complex and technical products, (4) the emergence of global markets, and (5) an economic period marked by low inflation.

6. **Understand and explain the project life cycle, its stages, and the activities that typically occur at each stage in the project.** The project life cycle is a mechanism that links time to project activities and refers to the stages in a project's development. The common stages used to describe the life cycle for a project are (1) conceptualization, (2) planning, (3) execution, and (4) termination. A wide and diverse set of activities occurs during different life cycle stages; for example, during the conceptualization phase, the basic project mission and scope is developed and the key project stakeholders are signed on to support the project's development. During planning, myriad project plans and schedules are created to guide the development process. Execution requires that the principal work of the project be performed, and finally, during the termination stage, the project is completed, the work is finished, and the project is transferred to the customer.

7. **Understand the concept of project "success," including various definitions of success, such as the "triple constraint," as well as the alternative models of success.** Originally, project success was predicated simply on a triple constraint model that rewarded projects if they were completed with regard to schedule, budget, and functionality. This model ignored the emphasis that needed to be placed on project clients, however. In more accurate terms, project success involves a "quadruple constraint," linking the basic project metrics of schedule adherence, budget adherence, project quality (functionality), and customer satisfaction with the finished product. Other models of project success for IT projects employ the measures of (1) system quality, (2) information quality, (3) use, (4) user satisfaction, (5) individual impact, and (6) organizational impact.

8. **Understand the purpose of project management maturity models and the process of benchmarking in organizations.** Project management maturity models are used to allow organizations to benchmark the best practices of successful project management firms. Project maturity models recognize that different organizations are at different levels of sophistication in their best practices for managing projects. The purpose of benchmarking is to systematically manage the process improvements of project delivery by a single organization over a period of time. As a firm commits to implementing project management practices, maturity models offer a helpful, multistage process for moving forward through increasing levels of sophistication of project expertise.

9. **Identify the relevant maturity stages that organizations go through to become proficient in their use of project management techniques.** While there are a number of project maturity models, several of the most common share some core features. For example, most take as their starting point the assumption that unsophisticated organizations initiate projects in an ad hoc fashion, with little overall shared knowledge or procedures. As the firm moves through intermediate steps, it will begin to initiate processes and project management procedures that diffuse a core set of project management techniques and cultural attitudes throughout the organization. Finally, the last stage in maturity models typically recognizes that by this point the firm has moved beyond simply learning the techniques of project management and is working at continuous improvement processes to further refine, improve, and solidify project management philosophies among employees and departments.

Key Terms

Benchmarking *(p. 18)*
Client acceptance *(p. 15)*
Clients *(p. 13)*
Cost *(p. 15)*

Deliverables *(p. 5)*
Performance *(p. 15)*
Process *(p. 4)*
Project *(p. 4)*

Project life cycle *(p. 12)*
Project management *(p. 8)*
Project management maturity models *(p. 18)*

Project success *(p. 15)*
Stakeholders *(p. 12)*
Time *(p. 15)*
Triple constraint *(p. 15)*

Discussion Questions

1. What are some of the principal reasons why project management has become such a popular business tool in recent years?
2. What do you see as being the primary challenges to introducing a project management philosophy to most organizations? That is, why is it difficult to shift to a project-based approach in many companies?
3. What are the advantages and disadvantages to using project management?
4. What are the key characteristics all projects possess?
5. Describe the basic elements of a project life cycle. Why is an understanding of the life cycle relevant for our understanding of projects?
6. Think of a successful project and an unsuccessful project with which you are familiar. What distinguishes the two, both in terms of the process used to develop them and their outcomes?
7. Consider the Expedition Everest case: What are the elements in Disney's approach to developing its theme rides that you find particularly impressive? How can a firm like Disney balance the need for efficiency and smooth development of projects with the desire to be innovative and creative? Based on this case, what principles appear to guide its development process?
8. Consider the six criteria for successful IT projects. Why is IT project success often so difficult to assess? Make a case for some factors being more important than others.
9. As organizations seek to become better at managing projects, they often engage in benchmarking with other companies in similar industries. Discuss the concept of benchmarking. What are its goals? How does benchmarking work?
10. Explain the concept of a project management maturity model. What purpose does it serve?
11. Compare and contrast the four project management maturity models shown in Table 1.3. What strengths and weaknesses do you perceive in each of the models?

Case Study 1.1

MegaTech, Inc.

MegaTech, Inc. designs and manufactures automotive components. For years, the company enjoyed a stable marketplace, a small but loyal group of customers, and a relatively predictable environment. Though slowly, annual sales continued to grow until recently hitting $300 million. MegaTech products were popular because they required little major updating or yearly redesign. The stability of its market, coupled with the consistency of its product, allowed MegaTech to forecast annual demand accurately, to rely on production runs with long lead times, and to concentrate on internal efficiency.

Then, with the advent of the North American Free Trade Agreement (NAFTA) and other international trade agreements, MegaTech found itself competing with auto parts suppliers headquartered in countries around the world. The company was thrust into an unfamiliar position: It had to become customer-focused and quicker to market with innovative products. Facing these tremendous commercial challenges, top management at MegaTech decided a few years ago to recreate the company as a project-based organization.

The transition, while not smooth, has nonetheless paid big dividends. Top managers determined, for instance, that product updates had to be much more frequent. Achieving this goal meant yearly redesigns and new technologies, which, in turn, meant making innovative changes in the firm's operations. In order to make these adjustments, special project teams were formed around each of the company's product lines and given a mandate to maintain market competitiveness.

At the same time, however, MegaTech wanted to maintain its internal operating efficiencies. Thus all project teams were given strict cost and schedule guidelines for new product introductions. Finally, the company created a sophisticated research and development team, which is responsible for locating likely new avenues for technological change 5 to 10 years down the road. Today, MegaTech operates project teams not only for managing current product lines but also for seeking longer-term payoffs through applied research.

MegaTech has found the move to project management challenging. For one thing, employees are still rethinking the ways in which they allocate their time and resources. In addition, the firm's success rate with new projects is still less than management had hoped. Nevertheless, top managers feel that, on balance, the shift to project management has given the company the operating advantage that it needed to maintain its lead over rivals in its globally competitive industry. "Project management," admits one MegaTech executive, "is certainly not a magic pill for success, but it has started us thinking about how we operate. As a result, we are doing smarter things in a faster way around here."

Questions

1. What is it about project management that offers MegaTech a competitive advantage in its industry?
2. What elements of the marketplace in which MegaTech operates led the firm to believe that project management would improve its operations?

Case Study 1.2

The IT Department at Hamelin Hospital

Hamelin Hospital is a large (700-bed) regional hospital in the northeastern United States. The information technology (IT) department employs 75 people and has an operating budget of over $35 million. The department is responsible for managing 30–40 projects, ranging from small (redesigning computer screens) to very large, such as multimillion-dollar system development projects that can run for over a year. Hamelin's IT department has been growing steadily, reflecting the hospital's commitment to expanding its information storage and processing capacities. The two principal functions of the IT department are developing new software applications and maintaining the current information system. Project management is a way of life for the department.

IT department jobs fall into one of five categories: (1) help-desk technician, (2) programmer, (3) senior programmer, (4) systems analyst, and (5) project manager. Help-desk technicians field queries from computer system users and solve a wide range of problems. Most new hires start at the help desk, where they can become familiar with the system, learn about problem areas, become sensitive to users' frustrations and concerns, and understand how the IT department affects all hospital operations. As individuals move up the ladder, they join project teams, either as programmers or systems analysts. Finally, five project managers oversee a constantly updated slate of projects. In addition, the workload is always being supplemented by new projects. Team personnel finish one assignment and then move on to a new one. The typical IT department employee is involved in seven projects, each at a different stage of completion.

(continued)

The project management system in place at Hamelin is well regarded. It has spearheaded a tremendous expansion of the hospital's IT capabilities and thus helped it to gain a competitive advantage over other regional hospitals. Recently, in fact, Hamelin began "farming out" its IT services on a fee-for-service basis to competing hospitals needing help with their records, administration, order entry systems, and so forth. Not surprisingly, the results have improved the hospital's bottom line: At a time when more and more health care organizations are feeling the effects of spiraling health care costs, Hamelin's IT department has helped the hospital sustain continuous budget increases, additional staffing, a larger slate of projects, and a track record of success.

Questions

1. What are the benefits and drawbacks of starting most new hires at the help desk function?
2. What are the potential problems with requiring project team members to be involved in multiple projects at the same time? What are the potential advantages?
3. What signals does the department send by making "project manager" the highest position in the department?

Internet Exercises

1. The largest professional project management organization in the world is the Project Management Institute (PMI). Go to its Web site, www.pmi.org and examine the links you find. What are some of the links that suggest that project management has become a sophisticated and vital element in corporate success? Select at least three of the related links and report briefly on the content of these links.
2. Go to the PMI Web site and examine the link "Global Membership and Communities." What do you discover when you begin navigating among the various chapters and cooperative organizations associated with PMI? How does this information cause you to rethink project management as a career option?
3. Type www.pmi.org/AboutUs/Pages/case-study-library.aspx into your browser. Examine some of the cases included on the resulting page. What do they suggest about the challenges of managing projects successfully? The complexity of many of today's projects? The exciting breakthroughs or opportunities that projects allow us to exploit?
4. Using your favorite search engine (Google, Yahoo!, etc.), type in the keywords "project" and "project management." Randomly select three of the links that come up on the screen. Summarize what you found.
5. Go to the Web site for the Software Engineering Institute of Carnegie Mellon University at www.sei.cmu.edu/pub/documents/94.reports/pdf/sr07.94.pdf and access the software process maturity questionnaire. What are some of the questions that IT companies need to consider when assessing their level of project management maturity?
5. Go to the Prentice Hall Companion Web site supporting this text, www.prenhall.com/pinto. Internet Reading: Morris, P. W. G. (1998), "Why project management doesn't always make business sense," *Project Management*, 4 (1), 12–16.
6. Go to the Prentice Hall Web site supporting this text, www.prenhall.com/pinto. Internet Reading: Cook, C. R., and Pritchard, C. L. (1998), "Why project management?" in D. I. Cleland (Ed.), *The Project Management Field Guide*. New York: Van Nostrand Reinhold, pp. 22–33.

PMP Certification Sample Questions

1. The majority of the project budget is expended upon:
   a. Project plan development.
   b. Project plan execution.
   c. Project termination.
   d. Project communication.

2. Which of the following is the most critical component of the triple constraint?
   a. Time, then cost, then quality.
   b. Quality, then cost, then time.
   c. Scope.
   d. They are all of equal importance unless otherwise stated.

3. Which of the following best describes a project stakeholder?
   a. A team member.
   b. The project manager.
   c. Someone who works in an area affected by the project.
   d. All of the above are stakeholders.

4. All of the following are elements in the definition of a project, except:
   a. A project is time limited.
   b. A project is unique.
   c. A project is composed of unrelated activities.
   d. A project is undertaken for a purpose.

5. All of the following distinguish project management from other process activities, except:
   a. There are no fundamental differences between project and process management.
   b. Project management often involves greater certainty of performance, cost, and schedule.
   c. Process management operates outside of line organizations.
   d. None of the above correctly distinguish project from process management.

Answers: 1. b—The majority of a project budget is spent during the execution phase; 2. d—Unless otherwise stated, all elements in the triple constraint are equally critical; 3. d—All of the examples listed are types of project stakeholder; 4. c—A project is composed of "interrelated" activities; 5. d—None of the answers given correctly differentiates "process" from "project" management.

Notes

1. Valery, Paul, quoted in "Extreme Chaos" (2001), The Standish Group International.
2. Jenkins, Robert N. (2005), "A new peak for Disney," St. Petersburg Times Online, www.sptimes.com/2005/12/11/news_pf/travel/A_new_peak_for_Disney
3. Peters, Thomas (1994), *Liberation Management: Necessary Disorganization for the Nanosecond Nineties.* New York: Fawcett Books.
4. Stewart, Thomas H. (1995), "The corporate jungle spawns a new species," *Fortune,* July 10, pp. 179–80.
5. Gilbreath, Robert D. (1988), "Working with pulses not streams: Using projects to capture opportunity," in Cleland, D. and King, W. (Eds.), *Project Management Handbook.* New York: Van Nostrand Reinhold, pp. 3–15.
6. Buchanan, D. A. and Boddy, D. (1992), *The Expertise of the Change Agent: Public Performance and Backstage Activity.* London: Prentice Hall.
7. Frame, J. D. (1995), *Managing Projects in Organizations,* 2nd ed. San Francisco, CA:. Jossey-Bass. See also, Frame, J. D. (2002), *The New Project Management,* 2nd ed. San Francisco, CA: Jossey-Bass.
8. Kerzner, H. (2003), *Project Management,* 8th ed. New York: Wiley.
9. Field, M. and Keller, L. (1998), *Project Management.* London: The Open University.
10. Project Management Institute (2000), *A Guide to the Project Management Body of Knowledge.* Newtown Square, PA: PMI.
11. Cleland, D. I. (2001), "The discipline of project management," in J. Knutson (Ed.), *Project Management for Business Professionals.* New York: John Wiley and Sons, pp. 3–22.
12. Lundin, R. A. and Soderholm, A. (1995), "A theory of the temporary organization," *Scandinavian Journal of Management,* 11(4): 437–55.
13. Graham, R. J. (1992), A survival guide for the accidental project manager. *Proceedings of the Annual Project Management Institute Symposium.* Drexel Hill, PA: Project Management Institute, 355–61.
14. Sources: http://macs.about.com/b/a/087641.htm; Mossberg, W. S., (2004), "The Music Man," *Wall Street Journal,* June 14, p. B1.
15. Pinto, J. K. and Millet, I. (1999), *Successful Information Systems Implementation: The Human Side,* 2nd ed. Newtown Square, PA: PMI.
16. Kapur, G. K. (1998), Don't look back to create the future. Presentation at the *Frontiers of Project Management Conference,* Boston, MA.
17. *CIO* (1995), Editorial. Nov. 15, p. 5.
18. "How to establish an organizational culture that promotes projects," www.bia.ca/articles/HowToEstablishaProjectManagementCulture.htm; Standish Group (2006), *The Trends in IT Value* report.
19. Kelley, M. (2008), "$600M spent on canceled contracts," *USA Today,* November 18, p. 1.
20. Cleland, D. I. (1994), *Project Management: Strategic Design and Implementation.* New York: McGraw-Hill; Pinto, J. K. and Rouhiainen, P. (2001), *Building Customer-Based Project Organizations.* New York: John Wiley and Sons; Gray, C. F. and Larson, E. W. (2003), *Project Management,* 2nd ed. Burr Ridge, IL: McGraw-Hill.
21. Petroski, H. (1985), *To Engineer Is Human—The Role of Failure in Successful Design.* London: St. Martin's Press.
22. http://en.wikipedia.org/wiki/Dubailand, "Projects in Dubai," www.skidubai.com/dubai/projects/, "Dubai Projects," www.funonthenet.in/content/view/127/31/, "Falcon City of Wonders, Dubai," March 27, 2008, http://uaemegaprojects.blogspot.com/
23. Sohmen, Victor (2002), "Project termination: Why the delay?" Paper presented at PMI Research Conference 2002, Seattle, WA, July.
24. Freeman, M. and Beale, P. (1992), "Measuring project success," *Project Management Journal,* vol. 23(1), pp. 8–17.
25. Morris, P. W. G. (1997), *The Management of Projects.* Thomas Telford: London; "Women design concept car for Volvo," www.usatoday.com/money/autos/2004-03-02; "This Volvo is not a guy thing," http://www.businessweek.com/magazine/04_11, March 15, 2004.
26. Shenhar, A. J., Levy, O., and Dvir, D. (1997), "Mapping the dimensions of project success," *Project Management Journal,* vol. 28(2), pp. 5–13.
27. DeLone, W. H. and McLean, E. R. (1992), "Information systems success: The quest for the dependent variable," *Information Systems Research,* 3(1), pp. 60–95; Seddon, P. B. (1997), "A respecification and extension of the DeLone and McLean model of IS success," *Information Systems Research,* 8(3), pp. 249–53; DeLone, W. H. and McLean, E. R. (2003), "The DeLone and McLean model of information system success: A ten-year update," *Journal of Management Information Systems,* 19(4), pp. 9–30.
28. Atkinson, R. (1999), "Project management: Cost, time and quality, two best guesses and a phenomenon, it's time to accept other success criteria," *International Journal of Project Management,* 17(6), pp. 337–42; Cooke-Davies, T. (2002), "The 'real' success factors on projects," *International Journal of Project Management,* 20(3), pp. 185–190; Olson, D. L. (2001), *Introduction to Information Systems Project Management.* Burr Ridge, IL: Irwin/McGraw-Hill.
29. Pennypacker, J. S. and Grant, K. P. (2003), Project management maturity: An industry benchmark, *Project Management Journal,* 34(1), 4–11; Ibbs, C. W. and Kwak, Y. H. (1998), "Benchmarking project management organizations," *PMNetwork,* 12(2), 49–53.
30. Reginato, P. E. and Ibbs, C. W. (2002), Project management as a core competency, *Proceedings of PMI Research Conference 2002,* Slevin, D., Pinto, J., and Cleland, D. (Eds.). Newtown Square, PA: Project Management Institute, 445–50.
31. Crawford, K. (2002), *Project Management Maturity Model: Providing a Proven Path to Project Management Excellence,* New York: Marcel Dekker; Foti, R. (2002), "Implementing maturity models," *PMNetwork,* 16(9), 39–43; Gareis, R., (2001), "Competencies in the project-oriented organization," in Slevin, D., Cleland, D., and Pinto, J., *The Frontiers of Project Management Research.* Newtown Square, PA: Project Management Institute, 213–24; Gareis, R. and Huemann, M. (2000), "Project management competencies in the project-oriented organization," in Turner, J. R. and Simister, S. J. (Eds.), *The Gower Handbook of Project Management,*

3rd ed., Aldershot, UK: Gower, 709–22; Ibbs, C. W. and Kwak, Y. H. (2000), "Assessing project management maturity," *Project Management Journal,* 31(1), 32–43.

32. Humphrey, W. S. (1988), "Characterizing the software process: A maturity framework," *IEEE Software,* vol. 5(3), pp. 73–79; Carnegie Mellon University, (1995), *The Capability Maturity Model: Guidelines for Improving the Software Process,* Boston, MA: Addison-Wesley; Kerzner, H. (2001), *Strategic Planning for Project Management Using a Project Management Maturity Model,* New York: Wiley; Crawford, J. K., (2002), *Project Management Maturity Model,* New York: Marcel Dekker; Pritchard, C. (1999), *How to Build a Work Breakdown Structure: The Cornerstone of Project Management,* Arlington, VA: ESI International.

SMC Students, Welcome to myitlab!

Your instructor has chosen to use **myitlab** as a component of your course. Designed to help you succeed in your course, myitlab provides you with a training and testing environment for Microsoft Office applications, computer skills, and computer concepts.

To access your **myitlab** online course for the first time, you need to register *and* log in. Whenever you want to use **myitlab** after that, you just need to log in. You can do both from the same starting point, at www.myitlab.com

To register for myitlab

To register, you will need
1. A valid email address_____
2. myitlab student access code: _____
3. your school's zip code: **90405**_____
4. Course ID from your instructor_____

If you purchased a new textbook, it should have come with a Student Access Kit that contains a code you can use to register. If you do not have a Student Access Kit, you can purchase access online with a major credit card.

1. Start Internet Explorer and go to www.myitlab.com. Click the **Student button**, under **First-Time Users**.
2. Agree to the License Agreement and terms by clicking **I Accept**
3. On the **Access Information** page, you will be asked if you have a Pearson Education account. If **Yes**, enter the existing login name and password.
4. If you do not have an account, click the **No** option, and enter your desired login name and password. Re-type your password.
5. Enter your **Access Code** from the **myitlab Student Access Kit**.
6. On the **Account Information** page, enter your first and last name and email.
7. In the **School Location** section, select your country and enter your school's **ZIP** or **postal code**. Select your school from the list.
8. Select a **Security Question** and enter the answer. Click **Next**.
9. A **Confirmation and Summary** page displays, indicating your registration is successful! This information will also be emailed to you.
10. Click **Log in Now** to log into myitlab.
11. On the **My Courses** page, click **Enroll in a Course** and type the **Course ID** provided to you by your instructor—it will be similar to this: CRSABQW—123456
12. On the **Confirm Course** page verify the course and instructor are correct. Click **Submit**, and then **Enter Course Now.**

To log into myitlab

1. Go to http://www.myitlab.com
2. Enter the personal user name and password you just created, and click **Log In.** Click the **Course Name** to enter your course.

Need More Help?

Additional help can be found at www.myitlab.com on the Support tab, under Student Support.